Napoleon III
and Mexican Silver

Napoleon III
and Mexican Silver

Shirley J. Black

Ferrell Publications
Silverton, Colorado

It has often been said that men are blind to their own times. To be generous, let us say that they are merely very short-sighted…. but perhaps we can define the process more clearly by noting that among the whole range of human activity there are certain areas in which blindness or myopia of contemporaries is particularly noticeable: at the head of the list come economic events.

—*Marcel Blanchard**

* Marcel Blanchard, "The Railway Policy of the Second Empire," in F. Crouzet, W. H. Chaloner, and W. M. Stern, eds., *Essays in European Economic History, 1789-1914,* (New York: St. Martin's, 1969), p. 98.

Table of Contents

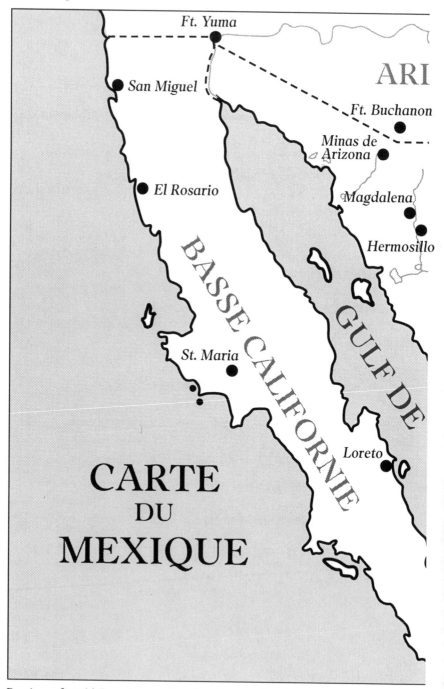

ARI

Ft. Yuma

San Miguel

Ft. Buchanon

Minas de
Arizona

El Rosario

Magdalena

Hermosillo

BASSE CALIFORNIE

GULF DE

St. Maria

Loreto

CARTE
DU
MEXIQUE

Portion of 1864 French map showing Sonora, Sinaloa, Durango, Chihuahua

Map • ix

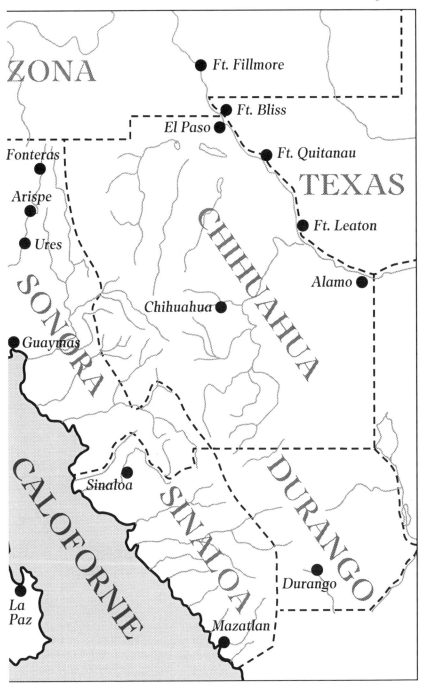

and Lower California. (Senate Ex. Doc. No. 11, 33rd Cong. 2nd Sess.)

Preface

Much of this study by Shirley J. Black appeared in 1974 as a doctoral dissertation. That format also included a number of appendices presenting statistical information regarding prices and the ebb and flow of gold, silver, cotton and other commodities on world markets. It is available from University Microfilms International at Ann Arbor, Michigan.

A version also appeared in 1974 in the first issue of the *Proceedings* of the Western Society for French History. It had been presented as a paper at that society's founding meeting in Flagstaff, Arizona. On that occasion Albert Soboul remarked, "Finally we have an economic interpretation of the intervention that really makes sense." Indeed, to that point economic explanations of the French intervention in Mexico were limited to the immediate background of the Tripartite Convention, to the welfare of French and other European residents in Mexico City, or to the Jecker bonds. Even one brief consideration of Napoleon III's interest in Mexico's mineral resources never related this to the bimetallic crisis in France.

After 1974 Black continued her study and wrote a number of academic papers and articles. A truncated version of her findings appeared in the *Revue historique* (CCLIX – 1978, No. 1, pp. 55-73) entitled, "Napoléon III et le Mexique: un triomphe monétaire." By the time of her death in September 1996, she had nearly completed a revision of her entire study which, with minor modifications, constitutes this book.

Meanwhile she had started an extensive study of Louis Napoleon's abortive 1836 Strasbourg coup. The final corpus of her work includes a penetrating preliminary article on this subject* as well as an article

---

* "The Strasbourg *Coup:* The Napoleonic Legend in Action," *The Consortium on Revolutionary Europe: Proceedings,* XVII (1987), pp. 491-504.

on the disputed status of Olivenza, subsequently republished in Spain.**

A word of special thanks is due a host of librarians, archivists and special friends who gave unstintingly of their time and expertise in the furtherance of this study of the French intervention in Mexico. Particular mention should be made of Duane Roller and Alice Timmons at the University of Oklahoma, Berta Ulloa at El Colegio de Mexico, Carolyn Sung at the Library of Congress and R. John Rath, formerly of Rice University.

I am responsible for the final editorial revisions of the manuscript. These involved a bit of rewriting, deletion of some material formerly in appendices, and incorporation of the findings of Shirley's later research. I hope she would have approved this final version of her work.

Brison D. Gooch

** "Olivenza: An Iberian 'Alsace-Lorraine,' " *The Americas*, XXXV/4 (April, 1979) pp. 527-37, reprinted as "Olivenza: una 'Alsacia Lorena' iberica," in *Encuentros: Revista luso-espanola de investigadores en Ciencias Humanas y Sociales*, Olivenza, 1997, No. 3, pp. 241-58.

Chapter One

Introduction

————•—————

The French intervention in Mexico has defied simple explanation. Even Napoleon III complained, "The interest which we may have in creating a great Empire in Mexico has never been fully appreciated in France."[1] After researching the causes of the expedition for more than twenty-five years, two prominent twentieth century historians agreed that the French emperor's action had perplexed not only contemporaries but also historians for over a century.[2]

Some scholars have simply assumed that it was an imperialistic move, typical of a Bonaparte, to gain prestige and to solidify popularity by a dramatic foreign policy, in bold contrast to the earlier vacillation of the Orleanist king, Louis Philippe. This scenario, however, is inadequate. Most Frenchmen were either antagonistic or disinterested in the enterprise, yet Napoleon III persevered. For some, the expedition aroused scornful derision and allusions to Mexico as the Moscow of the Second Empire. Nonetheless, Napoleon firmly continued to maintain and to augment his troops across the Atlantic, even when the American Civil War was ending. The question is, why?

Historians have proposed various theories which have long been in the realm of common knowledge: Napoleon's defense of monarchism in the Western Hemisphere by adding French influence to that of the Russian, British, Dutch, Spanish, and Portuguese; commercial advantages to France through canal building and a Central American empire; the persistent persuasions of Mexican monarchists; the

---

1. Napoleon III to Maximilian, April 12, 1866, Count Egon Caesar Corti, *Maximilian and Charlotte of Mexico*, 2 vols. (New York: Alfred A. Knopf, 1929), II, 934.
2. Alfred Jackson Hanna and Kathryn Abbey Hanna, *Napoleon III and Mexico: American Triumph Over Monarchy* (Chapel Hill: University of North Carolina Press, 1971), p. 3

intrigues of French diplomats; the pressures of "priests and petti-coats": the influence of the Empress Eugénie and of the Catholic church in obstructing Protestant American expansion; compensation to the Hapsburgs for earlier French opposition to Austrian hegemony in Italy; Mexico's instability that culminated in the moratorium on foreign debts; the Mexican investments of Jean Baptiste Jecker, the Duc de Morny, and powerful French financiers; defiance of the Monroe Doctrine during the vulnerable era of the American Civil War in order to curtail future expansion by the United States; Napoleon's romantic interest in Latin America that dated back to his days in the prison at Ham; and a concatenation of events that simply pushed Napoleon forward, from crisis to crisis, in an effort to avenge the defeat at Puebla and to acquire glory for France.

Such simple ideas could hardly be expected to account for a complex foreign policy, but in this case all of these factors have some element of truth. Cumulatively, however, they do not sufficiently justify the momentous decision to send thousands of French troops to Mexico and to sustain them there for five years. The question has remained: why would Napoleon III spend millions of francs to establish a Hapsburg on a remote throne? This study explores the French intervention in Mexico in the context of Napoleon's dire need for silver to relieve pressing monetary and economic problems in France. Whatever other considerations there may have been, documents and statistics indicate that a French dearth of silver was a primary reason for the intervention.

Since he had become emperor, Napoleon had been plagued by problems stemming from an unprecedented influx of gold from America and Australia. This gold upset the French bimetallic monetary standard and resulted in mass exports of silver from France. The need for silver became even more intense in 1861 when the American Civil War began. Cotton suppliers in India, replacing producers in the United States, demanded payment in silver, the very metal that the French emperor lacked. Thus, stimulated by the specter of unemployment and mass discontent in the textile industry, Napoleon decided that the silver mines of Mexico would alleviate his nation's monetary, economic, and social distress.

Napoleon's interest in Mexican silver can be traced through French attempts to obtain a lien on the mines of Sonora, reputedly one of the richest but most vulnerable areas in Mexico. A few contemporaries were keenly aware of this. Eugène Lefêvre, a French journalist and political opponent of the Second Empire, asserted that Napoleon's eagerness to control Sonora's mines was a major cause of the expedition.[3] Even before overt French moves towards northern Mexico, Senator James A. McDougall of California pointed out that France had no "home supply" of precious metals and alerted his countrymen that Napoleon had designs on Sonora.[4] And Francisco Zarco, a former Mexican minister of foreign affairs, claimed that Mexico's mineral wealth was "the magnet of the expedition, the first cause of the intense interest Napoleon takes in Mexico, and the great argument of his ministers to justify his crimes before the legislative assembly."[5]

The poet-politician Alphonse Lamartine, foreign minister in the early months of the Second Republic and later defeated by Louis Napoleon in a bid for the presidency, eloquently protested that his country's intervention in Mexico was "misunderstood." While others feared Napoleonic imperialism, Lamartine worriedly noted the imperialistic expansion of the United States: "Who does not know that the monetary capital of the universe is in the immense mines . . . [which] will place all the capital in gold and silver of the universe in the hands of the United States . . . ?" This menacing possibility, he claimed, was "the secret thought which inspired the Mexican expedition."[6]

Lamartine's alarm was not fanciful. Before gold discoveries in South Africa in 1885, the world's major source of precious metals was in the Western Hemisphere. Europeans uneasily believed that the United States, already controlling a massive portion of gold-bearing territory, might expand southward and obtain additional mineral-rich areas. Lamartine feared that Americans would then become "masters" of the

---

3. Eugène Lefêvre, ed., *Documents officiels recueillis dans la secrétaire privée de Maximilien. Histoire de l'intervention française au Mexique,* 2 vols. (Brussels: 1869), II, 91.
4. Speech, February 3, 1863, recorded in the *Congressional Globe,* 37th Cong., 3rd sess., appendix, p. 97.
5. Article by Francisco Zarco, *La Acción,* Saltillo, June 18, 1864, in Romero to Seward, July 12, 1864, U.S., Department of State, *Diplomatic Correspondence,* 1865, 39th Cong., 1st sess., pt. 3, p. 581.
6. Article by Alphonse Lamartine, *Les Entretiens Littéraires,* November 1865, ibid., pp. 662-64.

price of gold and silver and this, in turn, would result in their being "masters" of Europe's vital industries.7 In the fifty years from 1803 to 1853, the United States had expanded tremendously, acquiring the Louisiana Territory from France, Florida from Spain, the Oregon Territory from England, and almost one-half of Mexico. Few expected that the boundaries would remain stationary in the succeeding fifty years.

These contemporary accounts were essentially correct, as far as they went. They portrayed Napoleon either as simply greedy for Mexican mines, without fathoming his great need for silver, or as a self appointed gendarme, altruistically saving Europe from the United States' control over the world's vital source of precious metals. For many reasons, Napoleon could not publicly articulate his own policy. Partly because of the resulting ambiguities, the imperatives which drove him to Mexico escaped both the general public and historians of the Second Empire, although almost all accounts mention the silver mines of Sonora as a gratuitous by-product of the intervention. Had he candidly admitted his reasons for sending troops to Mexico, the hostility of Great Britain and the United States would have been dangerously aroused, as both also had interests in Sonora and in Mexican silver.

It is small wonder that American hostility to the French intervention in Mexico exasperated and angered Napoleon III. Both his severe monetary dilemma and his critical economic problems emanated from the United States: the production of California gold and the cessation of Confederate cotton supplies forcing him into a search for silver.

---

7. Ibid.

Chapter Two

The Legend of Silver in Sonora

———•———

The imbalance in the French bimetallic system resulting from the massive influx of gold during the 1850s prompted Napoleon III to seek additional silver. For centuries Mexico had been the world's major producer of that metal. Nature had endowed the Mexican state of Sonora with particularly rich silver deposits, and these had only been partially mined.[1] Thus the answer to the French emperor's needs appeared to be largely unattended and ignored in a desolate area in northwestern Mexico.

Envy of Mexican mines, which produced an estimated 75 percent of Mexico's total export value, was longstanding. Since the sixteenth-century conquest of Mexico by Hernando Cortés, there had been daring attempts to capture the annual Spanish treasure fleets from Vera Cruz to Seville and Cadiz, as ships under the flag of Castile were coveted by both pirates and princes. When Spanish kings were losing other possessions, they tenaciously held on to their New World mineral wealth. The early nineteenth century, however, brought merciless attacks. Because of the vulnerability of Spain's monarchy and the venality of the Prince of Peace, Napoleon Bonaparte almost succeeded in diverting Mexican silver to Paris.[2] And when scarcity of coin forced the Bank of England to stop specie payments, the French emigré general, Charles-François

———

1. Hubert Howe Bancroft, *History of California, 1848-1859* 7 vols., (San Francisco: History Co., 1888), VI, 583. For a recent penetrating analysis, see Richard L. Garner "Long-Term Silver Mining Trends in Spanish America: A Comparative Analysis of Peru and Mexico," *American Historical Review* 93, (October 1988): 898-935.
2. Georges Lefebvre, *Napoleon*, 2 vols. (New York: Columbia University Press, 1969), I , 232-37.

Dumouriez, urged England to strike a blow at both Spain and Napoleon by seizing the resources of Mexico.[3] A more subtle menace existed in the fledgling United States. While negotiating the Treaty of Paris in 1783, the Spanish Count de Aranda had predicted that this new nation would take Florida, and after thus becoming master of the Gulf of Mexico, then would try to conquer the vast empire of New Spain.[4]

In the decade from 1851 to 1861, Mexico's ability to resist foreign aggression waned. During these same years the French search for silver began to center on Sonora, seen to be in imminent danger of either conquest or secession. Sonora was somewhat like a mirage in that Napoleon III saw what he desperately wanted to see, the key to monetary resuscitation for France. By 1863, mining engineers believed that Sonora's mineral wealth was greater than that of any other Mexican state.[5]

In the decades preceding the French intervention in Mexico, numerous books and articles described the silver of Sonora. As early as 1794, the German Jesuit Ignaz Pfefferkorn cited eyewitnesses in an effort "to lift out of obscurity" this "very noteworthy" Mexican province. He claimed that Sonora's mines made it one of the most important areas in all Spanish America.[6] Dramatizing a mine at Cananea, he wrote, "Imagine a hall draped with tapestries interwoven with silver from top to bottom; so on all sides everything was streaked with pure silver."[7] Even that wealth was superceded in Primería Alta, which supposedly contained the most famous and richest silver mine yet discovered in Sonora and in all of New Spain since the conquest. This mine, claimed

---

3. *Wellington Supplementary Dispatches*, vol. 6, cited in "Mexico, by Baron Humboldt," *Catholic World* 7 (1868): 330.

4. "Memoria secreta presentada al rey Carlos III", José María Hidalgo, *Proyectos de monarquia en México* (México: F. Vázquez, 1904), p. 281.

5. Inge to Mowry, San Francisco, February 22, 1863, Sylvester Mowry, *Arizona and Sonora: The Geography, History, and Resources of the Silver Region of North America*, 3rd ed. rev. (New York: Harper & Bros., 1864), pp. 197-98.

6. Ignaz Pfefferkorn, *Sonora: A Description of the Province*, (Albuquerque: University of New Mexico Press, 1949), p. 21. First published in two volumes in 1794-95 as *Beschreibung der landschaft Sonora* at Köln am Rheine. Pfefferkorn was quoted in 1861 by Charles P. Stone who surveyed Sonora's public lands for Jean Baptiste Jecker; Charles P. Stone, "Notes on the State of Sonora," *Historical Magazine* 5 (June 1861): 168.

7. Pfefferkorn, *Sonora*, p. 89.

by Frenchmen in the 1850s near the village of Arizona, contained "a block of the finest silver, so large it had to be broken up with hammers and axes so that it could be removed." "Such a quantity of pure silver was found together here that it was doubtful whether it should be considered a mine or a depository of hidden treasures." In 1730, both Old and New Spain were astonished by the abundance of Sonora's silver.[8]

Pfefferkorn's allegations substantiated earlier views from the 1760s. When Nicolás de Lafora made an inspection tour, fundamental to the Marqués de Rubí's survey of New Spain's frontiers, he reported, "Virgin metals crop out everywhere in the hills and valleys" of Sonora.[9] And in 1769, the French ambassador to Spain, had written to his minister of foreign affairs that areas in northern New Spain "abound in mines of gold and silver."[10] News of the silver, allegedly only two or three feet deep in the earth, spread rapidly and, although "everything in and out of Sonora that had legs ran to the spot hoping to get rich quickly," local Apaches, Seris, and Pimas effectively terrorized the miners.[11] Accordingly, Sonora's mineral wealth, philosophically termed providential compensation for such "annoyances" as these frightening Indian attacks, was largely abandoned. Nearly one hundred years after Pfefferkorn's residence in Sonora, Jecker's surveyor noted the "crumbling walls" which marked past prosperity,[12] and Sylvester Mowry referred to "Infelix Sonora—most unhappy."[13] However, by the late eighteenth century the silver mining districts in southern Sonora, around Alamos, had some 6,280 persistent European settlers.[14]

Although Pfefferkorn had spent eleven years in Sonora, from 1756 to 1767, his objective of lifting Sonora out of obscurity was

---

8. Ibid., p. 90. Also see Hubert Howe Bancroft, *History of the North Mexican States and Texas*, 2 vols., (San Francisco: A. L. Bancroft, 1884), I, 525-28, and Eduardo W. Villa, *Historia del Estado de Sonora*, 2nd ed. (Hermosillo, Sonora: Editorial Sonora, 1951), p. 273.

9. Lawrence Kinnaird, ed., *The Frontiers of New Spain: Nicolás de Lafora's Description, 1766-1768* (Berkeley: Quivira Society, 1958), pp. 126-27.

10. Ossum to Choiseul in Mowry, *Arizona and Sonora*, pp. 39-40. A copy had been sent to Mowry by George Bancroft.

11. Pfefferfkorn, *Sonora*, p. 91.

12. Stone, "Sonora," 167.

13. Mowry, *Arizona and Sonora*, p. 31.

14. Roger Dunbier, *The Sonoran Desert: Its Geography, Economy, and People* (Tucson: University of Arizona Press, 1968), p. 151.

muted by timing.[15] The 1794 publication of his first volume coincided with startling European events: Louis XVI and Marie Antoinette had been executed the previous year, and revolutionary doctrines and war were spreading throughout the continent. In addition to Europe's preoccupation with problems far from Sonora, Pfefferkorn's expulsion from New Spain and imprisonment in Spain with other Jesuits subdued the reception to his writings. Though regarded as a Jesuit document, Ignaz Pfefferkorn's work was later cited extensively as proof of Sonoran silver wealth. It was a major publication preceding Alexander von Humboldt's massive five volumes on Mexico published in 1811. Von Humboldt had gone to Mexico in 1803 and spent a year there tediously studying the resources and records of Mexico. His work, like Pfefferkorn's, was overshadowed by momentous events: the 1810 Mexican rebellion against French control of Spain, and Napoleon's 1812 invasion of Russia. Spain's decrease in revenue after the Mexican war of independence seemed to reflect peninsular poverty; until the need for silver and the susceptibility of Mexico revived both interest and avarice regarding the minerals of her former colony.[16] For knowledge of this previous and potential wealth, Europeans turned to von Humboldt as the major source of information. Cited extensively, his works were the basis for interest in Mexico by both miners and ministers: "Humboldt in pieces has been dished up to suit all customers. An oyster could not be served in more varieties of style."[17]

The prolific statistics of Alexander von Humboldt showed that Mexico had provided two-thirds of the world's silver and, instead of being depleted by three centuries of Spanish mining, productivity had significantly increased since 1746. The north Mexican states of

---

15. Bancroft, *North Mexican States,* I, 564, 580.
16. "Mexico, by Baron Humboldt," 331. Also see Académie des sciences, *Comptes rendus hebdomadaires des séances de l'académie des sciences* 25 (1847): 160-63; and *Revue des cours scientifiques de la France et des l'étranger* 2 (1865): 374 ff., and 3 (1866): 62, 138, 175, 228, 250, 395, 512, 681-86, 738, 809-18.
17. "Mexico, by Baron Humboldt," 334 and "Review of Alexander de Humboldt's Travels," *Quarterly Review* 21 (1819): 320. The reviewer wryly commented that von Humboldt "never quits a subject till he has exhausted it." Von Humboldt's *Atlas géographique et physique du royaume de la Nouvelle Espagne* (Paris, 1811), was in Maximilian's personal library.

Sonora and Durango ranked second to central Mexico, the major mining area, in the Prussian geographer's grouping of principal silver mines listed according to the quantity of precious metals extracted. Sonora's mines were particularly alluring as they contained rare white silver; although their location, in deserted and savage areas, would require substantial colonization to provide better administration and a more industrious people to increase silver production. Von Humboldt predicted that if Mexico's mineral wealth were ever fully developed, "Europe would be again inundated, as in the sixteenth century, with silver"—language read with keen interest during the Second Empire when the French monetary system wavered from a dearth of silver. Sonora, with its sparse population, appeared to be a neglected and rich area that could offer France financial stability.[18]

The political problems of Mexico magnified its vulnerability. The economy was shattered by years of guerrilla warfare; and the productivity of the mines, Mexico's major source of revenue, decreased significantly. At Guanajuato, the area in which the independence movement began, mining production declined from 617,474 marks of silver in 1808 to 73,983 in 1821. Flooded mines and wrecked machinery were grim debris, and the silver production center began to shift northward, from Guanajuato and Zacatecas to Chihuahua, Durango, and Sonora. In an unrelenting cycle, Mexican prosperity demanded efficient mine productivity and the output of the mines commensurately depended on a stable political system. Europeans regarded Mexico as being economically paralyzed by short-term, high interest loans which required as collateral either customs duties or mortgages on government property.[19] Immigrants and freign investors slowly reactivated some mines; but when revolutions disrupted or endangered these enterprises, their appeals for intervention only heightened the instability.

18. "The Empire of Mexico" *Quarterly Review* 115 (April 1864): 356 based heavily on von Humboldt's work. Alexander von Humboldt, *Essai politique sur le royaume de la nouvelle espagne*, 5 vols. (Paris: Chez F. Schoell, 1811), II, 388-99; III, 12, 345-46, 357, 389; V, 15. Also see "Mines and Mining from 1500-1800," in Hubert Howe Bancroft, *History of Mexico, 1600-1803*, 6 vols., (San Francisco: A. L. Bancroft, 1883), III, 553-602. The white silver mines were also rich in lead. When von Humboldt was taking his notes, the intendancy of Sonora included Sinaloa.

19. "Empire of Mexico," 368, 380; and Bancroft, *History of Mexico*, VI, 505.

Nineteenth-century capitalists almost succeeded in garnering Mexican mineral wealth after three centuries of pirates, buccaneers, and smugglers had failed. Concerned about the faltering mining industry, in 1822 Mexico reduced duties on silver to one common tax of 3 percent; and in 1823 the government allowed foreign capital to enter legally when Congress permitted foreigners to become partial owners of Mexican mines, although they were stringently regulated and still restricted from owning real property. Lucas Alamán, Mexican minister of foreign relations, urgently tried to rehabilitate the mines in the 1820s by seeking French capital to form a Franco-Mexican mining company. When this effort was inadequate, he turned to British capital.[20] Although production of Mexican mines had precariously diminished, Europeans recalled the legends of vast treasures earlier discovered by Cortés and lucratively mined by Spaniards.

While a reviewer accused von Humboldt of "exuberance" over "the most common occurrences," his writings seem restrained when compared to an 1828 publication by Henry George Ward, British minister to Mexico.[21] Making an extensive survey of Mexico's economic resources, Ward spiritedly reported great potential mineral wealth, rekindling British interest in Mexican mines in the 1830s. An earlier speculative boom in British-Mexican mining companies ended with the panic of 1826, temporarily dampening British interest in Mexican mines. Complaining that von Humboldt's estimates on silver production were

20. Gilberto Crespo y Martínez, *México: La industria mineria, estudio de su evolución* (México: Oficina tip. de la Secretaría de fomento, 1903), pp. 66-67; and N. Ray Gilmore, "Henry George Ward, British Publicist for Mexican Mines," *Pacific Historical Review* 32 (February 1963):38. Alamán, from a prominent Mexican mining family, studied mineralogy in Paris and travelled in England, Germany, and the Low Countries before becoming Mexican representative in the Spanish Cortes. Maximilian's personal library included Lucas Alamán, *Historia de Méjico desde los primeros movimientos que prepararon su independencia en el año de 1808 hasta la época presente* (México, 1849).

21. "Review of Alexander de Humboldt's Travels," *Quarterly Review* 21 (1819): 320; and H[enry] G[eorge] Ward, *Mexico in 1827*, 2 vols. (London: Henry Colburn, 1828). Ward arrived in Mexico on March 11, 1825, as minister plenipotentiary to recognize Mexican independence; after concluding the treaty, he was Britain's first chargé d'affaires in Mexico. Maximilian's library included an 1828 Leipzig edition of Ward's *Gedrängtes Gemälde Zustandes von Mexiko im Jahre 1827.*

too conservative, Ward enabled Mexican mining stocks to find a responsive market in London. Spending three months in Sonora, the minister-mining publicist reported that a fellow Englishman there claimed that "almost every mountain and hill contains silver and gold."[22]

Ward noted the decrease of Mexican revenues since von Humboldt's publication and estimated that mining productivity had been reduced almost one-half after the Mexican insurrection of 1810. Cognizant that the *Essai politique* was the source of knowledge for most European enterprises in Mexico, he conscientiously pointed out to prospective investors new hazards that had emerged in the seventeen years after von Humboldt's work. Political disturbances, flooded mines, uncontrolled Indian depredations, disrupted communications, and the lack of investment capital were primary reasons for decreased mining activity and major deterrents to investment capital.[23]

These obstacles in Sonora, however, could be rationalized as manageable when weighed against prodigious rewards. Ward's statement that the untapped mines of Durango, Sonora, Chihuahua, and Sinaloa promised "riches superior to anything that Mexico has yet produced" was particularly seductive after von Humboldt's descriptions of Mexican mineral wealth. Not only were these riches in northern Mexico of a superior quality, but also, corroborating Pfefferkorn, they were allegedly

---

22. Arthur D. Gayer, William W. Rostow, et al., *The Growth and Fluctuation of the British Economy, 1790-1850,* 2 vols. (Oxford: Clarendon Press, 1953), I, 188-89. In 1824 Benjamin Disraeli invested in the Anglo-Mexican Mining Association and subsequently wrote three pamphlets praising Mexican mines. Robert Blake, *Disraeli* (New York: St. Martin's, 1967), pp. 24-26. See also Ward, *Mexico,* I, 25, 579; II, 136, 167-68 and his appendix C, "Notes on the State of Sonora and Cinaloa." Ward's volumes were almost verbatim from his official dispatches sent in answer to the British Foreign Office's 1826 request to accumulate information on Mexican mines. See Gilmore, "Henry George Ward," 35, 41, 44, 46. Colonel Bourne, an English investor in a Sonoran mine near Arispe, had prudently chosen as his partner Sonora's representative in the Mexican Senate.

23. Ward, *Mexico,* I, 361-62, 386, 428; II, 275. The *Medidas políticas,* probably written by José Mariá Morelos, had advocated the destruction of export potential, such as tobacco fields, mines, and sugar plantations. Wilbert H. Timmons, *Morelos: Priest, Soldier, Statesman of Mexico,* (El Paso: Western College Press, 1963), pp. 191-202. Archives used by von Humboldt were destroyed during civil disturbances. Ibid., pp. 8, 38. Also see "Report of the United Mexican Mining Association, March, 1827," in *Philosophical Magazine* 2 (July 1827): 71.

close to the surface, in contrast to greater depth and expenditures required for older mines in the southern districts. These easily obtained and supposedly superior minerals, "virgin" mines as Ward frequently termed them, were complemented by other advantages. Guaymas, "undoubtedly the best port in the Republic," had only about two thousand inhabitants, "very hospitable to strangers" and amazingly "protected" by a garrison of only thirty men. This vulnerability of northern Mexico was frequently referred to by French writers. Apache attacks were a major source of disquiet and decreased mining productivity. Although Ward noted that they had caused the rich silver mine of *Cobriza de San Felipe,* eight leagues north of Babacanora, to be abandoned, this was tempered by the observation that the mine was owned by two mere women; and furthermore, the Apaches possessed no firearms.[24]

Ward adopted the generally believed Mexican theory that the amount of silver increased toward the north, a supposition "confirmed by the superiority of all the Northern ores to those of the richest districts in the South." This idea, probably strengthened by the 1849 Californian discoveries, apparently originated in the eighteenth-century discovery of Sonora's *Bolas de Plata* mine of Arizona, which Pfefferkorn had enthusiastically described.[25] Mexicans themselves revived interest in the Arizona mine. A Mexican president's search of viceregal archives for references to this mine had turned up Philip V's decree, dated Aranjuez, May 28, 1741, which mentioned a mass of "pure silver" weighing 180 arrobas. From documents, mining experts, and personal observation, Ward was convinced that great mineral potential lay in the northern areas of Sonora, Sinaloa, Durango, and Chihuahua and that future mineral production there would "infinitely"

---

24. Ward, *Mexico,* I, 563, 569, 572; II, 127-28, 602 and Pfeffercorn, *Sonora,* p. 90. Although two women might be unable to withstand Apache arrows, men with military backgrounds—such as two emperors—could readily dismiss the hindrances described by Ward. This area of Babacanora [*sic*] is mentioned by Mowry, *Arizona and Sonora,* pp. 43-45, by Victor Adolphe Malte-Brun, *La Sonora et ses mines* (Paris: Arthus Bertrand, 1864), p. 27 (as Barbicanora), and by Captain Jim Box who reported that the "very rich" mine of Babicanora [*sic*] "was taken in hand by a company of French" in 1852 who continued to work the mine in 1861 "with great profit." Jim Box, "The Mines of Northern Mexico," *Knickerbocker Magazine* 57 (June 1861): 580.
25. Ward, *Mexico,* II, 136; Bancroft, *North Mexican States,* I, 526; Pfefferkorn, *Sonora,* p. 90; and Mowry, *Arizona and Sonora,* p. 174.

exceed that of the southern mines. Realizing that his statements might be considered exaggerated, Ward insisted, "They are not so; they will be confirmed by every future report."[26] Ward's influence was substantial. A French scientific expedition to northern Mexico during Maximilian's empire corroborated Ward and enthusiastically concluded that the "mother mountain" provided a "silver core" from which silver "radiated in all directions, growing less rich according to its distance from the centre." Such great wealth could compensate for both mining costs and army expenses as "five thousand men might dig, and pick, and blast away at it for a hundred years and at the end of that time the yield would be as rich, if not richer, than when they began." Claiming that Sonora was the most interesting area in all of Mexico, Ward provocatively asserted that its mines could provide Europeans with more wealth than had yet been discovered in the New World.[27]

---

26. Ward, *Mexico,* II, 136-38, 600. An *arroba* is 25.36 pounds. Ward obtained a "certified copy" of this decree. Thirty years after Ward's account, Stone wrote that one mass of silver from this mine weighed, "according to Jesuit records," 3,500 pounds, while Mowry reported one that weighed 3,600 pounds. Stone, "Sonora," 168; and Mowry, *Arizona and Sonora,* p. 174. Also see estimates of Malte-Brun, *La Sonora et ses mines,* p. 23; and Pfefferkorn, *Sonora,* pp. 90-91. Both mention this legendary mass of silver although assessment of the weight varies. However, a disillusioned investor, writing of Ward's influence—"Lo, were not the pages of Ward's *History of Mexico* unfolded to your gaze!"— bought $15,000 worth of stock in mines mentioned in Ward's *Mexico.* Relating the futility of investing in north Mexican mines, he amusingly concluded, "The first dollar I have ever received from any connection I have ever had with mines comes from this article narrating my experience." "My Mexican Mines," *Harper's New Monthly Magazine* 35 (September 1867): 457, 459, 462.
27. "Notice sur deux noveaux minéraux découverts à Culebras, au Mexique," *Annales des sciences naturelles* 14 (December 1827): 371-74; "Produit du Mexique en or et en argent monnayés," ibid. 16 (October 1829): 113; "State and Prospects of Mexico, 1845," *Eclectic* 6 (December 1845): 443; "The Mines of Santa Eulalia, Chihuahua," *Harper's New Monthly Magazine* 35 (November 1867): 685-86; and Ward, *Mexico,* II, 611. Ward persistently appealed to Europeans, since the United States also had aspirations. C. Harvey Gardiner, ed., *Mexico, 1825-1828: The Journal and Correspondence of Edward Thornton Tayloe* (Chapel Hill: University of North Carolina Press, 1959), p. 134. Tayloe was a staff member of Joel R. Poinsett, United States minister to Mexico and a bitter antagonist of H. G. Ward. Also see J. Fred Rippy, *Rivalry of the United States and Great Britain Over Latin America, 1808-1830* (Baltimore: Johns Hopkins Press, 1929).

British, French, and German capitalists, stimulated by the republication of von Humboldt's work and challenged by Ward's volumes, invested heavily in Mexican mines. This competition caused submission to terms dictated by Mexican proprietors, but constant litigation over disputed titles and fictitious claims hindered the enforcement of contracts. Mexico's political problems added further complications, while the lack of adequate transportation often resulted in expensive mining machinery never reaching its destination.[28] Attracted by the great mineral wealth described by von Humboldt and Ward, Europeans continued to believe that a stable and permissive Mexican government would reduce all these hindrances.

While European capital gradually revived the mines, Mexico continued to endure grave internal problems. In 1828 dissension again developed into civil war. When fighting in Mexico City destroyed the major shopping district, the Parian market, foreign residents were the main victims. Ferdinand VII of Spain, financially insolvent after losing the American colonies, believed that intervention in Mexico would restore order and sovereignty; and, in 1829, Spaniards seized the Mexican port of Tampico. Although Mexico repelled this invasion, the emerging pattern was clear: internal eruptions, damage to foreign investments, and attempted or threatened intervention.

With the secession of Texas, Mexico's weakness was abundantly apparent. In 1838, only two years after Texas became independent, the Orleanist monarch, Louis Philippe, demanded reimbursement for damages suffered by the French. Bombarding the hitherto impregnable fortress of San Juan de Ulúa, Louis Philippe's forces withdrew after securing a guarantee of claims valued at 600,000 pesos. This so called Pastry War, a Pyrrhic victory for Mexico, had lingering repercussions.[29]

---

28. "Empire of Mexico," 361-62.
29. The French were already a considerable number in Mexico. By 1854, nearly one-fourth of the 25,000 foreign residents were French. Wilfrid Hardy Calcott, *Santa Anna: The Story of an Enigma Who Once Was Mexico* (Norman: University of Oklahoma Press, 1936), p. 299. This incident is termed the Pastry War, as one of the French claimants was a baker at Tacubaya. For French accounts, see Pierre de la Gorce, *Histoire du second empire*, 12th ed., 7 vols. (Paris: Plon-Nourrit et cie, 1871), IV, 8-11; and Taxile Delord, *Histoire du second empire: 1848-1869*, 6 vols. (Paris: Librarie Germer Baillière, 1869-1875), III, 278-79.

Despite successfully coercing Mexico, Louis Philippe's foreign policy was generally cautious and contributed to his fall from power ten years later.[30] His successor, Napoleon III, had both a precedent for interference and a motivation for perseverance.

Throughout the 1840s and 1850s Mexico's troubles increased, as political and economic anarchy continued. Defying the central government, Yucatán boldly hired the navy of the new Texas Republic and, in 1848, offered its sovereignty to Spain, Great Britain, and the United States. Restless Indians in Sonora and Chihuahua became more assertive, and their relentless raids in the northern states provoked talk of secession by local liberals who despaired of government help. Both conservative and liberal Mexicans, imitating Europe and denigrating their own nation, sporadically sent out appeals for Europeans to restore order.[31] In 1840 José María Gutiérrez de Estrada first appealed for a monarch, and in 1853 Santa Anna and Lucas Alamán, trying to secure a tripartite intervention of Great Britain, Spain, and France in Mexico, endorsed Gutiérrez's interest in a Spanish prince.

The war with the United States was the most serious danger in Mexico's twenty-five years of independence. Desperation was apparent in 1846 when José María Luis Mora, the liberal Mexican minister to England, offered to sell Great Britain a portion of territory that would create a buffer between the United States and Mexico. Rivalry between Europe and the United States for northern Mexico was intense. Napoleon III was impressed by General Zachary Taylor's campaigns and by General Winfield Scott's march on Mexico City.

---

30. The Duc d'Aumale, fifth son of Louis Philippe, was later considered for the Mexican throne; and rumors were that even Louis Philippe coveted the Mexican crown. "Empire of Mexico," 377; and José Maria Hildalgo, *Notes secrètes de M. Hidalgo a développer le jour ou il conviendra d'écrire l'histoire de la foundation de l'empire mexicain* (Hausarchiv Kaiser Maximilians von Mexico, MSS in the Haus-Hof-und Staatsarchiv, Vienna, Photostatic Facsimiles, Library of Congress, Washington, carton 19, 1865, no. 46; hereinafter cited as HHUSA, Max.)

31. Nelson Reed, *The Caste War of Yucatan* (Stanford: Stanford University Press, 1967), pp. 31, 85-86. Robert C. Stevens, "The Apache Menace in Sonora, 1831-1849," *Arizona and the West* 6 (Autumn 1964): 211-22; Bancroft, *North Mexican States,* II, 671; and Nettie Lee Benson, "Mexican Monarchists, 1823-1867" (paper read at the Southwest Social Science Association, Dallas, Texas, March 23, 1973).

Within a mere two years after hostilities began, the United States absorbed more than one-half of Mexico in exchange for $15 million and the cancellation of unpaid claims. Annexation by the United States of northern Mexico, "in the direct 'manifest destiny' line of acquisition," seemed an attainable possibility.[32]

The further assailability of Mexico was patently recognized. In spite of earlier investment frustrations, during the 1850s—the period in which American and Australian gold was inundating Europe—European capital flooded into Mexican mining enterprises. In 1849 and 1850 Hippolyte du Pasquier de Dommartin, arriving in Mexico shortly after its abject defeat in the war with the United States, developed plans for French colonies, first in Chihuahua and then in Sonora. Delineating his objectives in a book published in 1852, Dommartin contributed to the developing rivalry of France and the United States for northern Mexico.[33] He claimed that French hegemony in Sonora would curtail further expansion of the United States, restore Sonora's prosperity, implant European Catholic colonists to stop advancing Anglo-Saxon Protestants and, while accomplishing these goals, the French would be remunerated with metallic wealth equivalent to that of California.[34] While requesting the cession of vast unoccupied lands "in order to offer it to my countrymen of France and of Europe," Dommartin cajoled, "A country calls us. . . . Let us go to her! And who knows but that in stretching out to her a hand of safety, we may, perhaps save ourselves."[35]

---

32. Charles A. Hale, *Mexican Liberalism in the Age of Mora, 1821-1853* (New Haven: Yale University Press, 1968), pp. 8, 15, 211; Calcott, *Santa Anna*, p. 303; and "Mines of Northern Mexico," 577.

33. Hippolyte du Pasquier de Dommartin, *Les États-Unis et le Mexique: l'intérêt européen dans l'Amérique du nord* (Paris: Gullaumin, 1852). For French evaluation of his plan, see *Annuaire des Deux Mondes, 1850* (Paris, 1851), pp. 909-10; for serialized translation of Dommartin's book see *New York Times*, December 15, 22, 24, 1852, and January 10, 1853. For congressional discussion of the Frenchman, see *Congressional Globe*, 32nd Cong., 2nd sess., vol. 26 (1853), appendix, pp. 91-92. Dommartin's book was reprinted in the *New York Times* after Napoleon III's coup d'état and after Count Raousset-Boulbon's occupation of Hermosillo in 1852.

34. This is a recurring prediction. See also Box, "Mines of Northern Mexico," 580; and Stone, "Sonora," 168.

35. *New York Times*, December 15, 1852.

Dommartin had substantial reasons for believing that Sonora would not only be receptive but also grateful to France. José de Aguilar, governor of Sonora, urgently contacted the French minister to Mexico, André Levasseur, to promote European immigration, and Sonora's 1850 colonization decree added substance to his sincerity.[36] Although Dommartin was discouraged when the Mexican central government rejected Sonora's colonization program, he was pensively hopeful that "if its fruit must be lost to me, I do not wish that it should be for my country." Ruminating on the riches of Mexico before 1810, he took samples of Sonora's mineral wealth back to France and explained that the major reason such silver had been neglected was the insufficiency of Mexicans to work the mines and defend their country at the same time. With great insistence—"As a European, as a Frenchman, I beseech Europe, I adjure my country"—Dommartin pleaded for prompt and vigorous intervention in northern Mexico.[37] Interest was heightened by the Mexican display at the Universal Exposition of 1855 in Paris where five million visitors, including sovereigns from central and western Europe, viewed Mexican products and considered them the most remarkable of the Western Hemisphere, after those from the United States. [38]

Dommartin's emotional persistence was vindicated by United States interest in Sonora. In February 1859, Sylvester Mowry alerted Frenchmen and others to rival designs when he addressed the American Geographical and Statistical Society in New York on the importance of Arizona and Sonora. Mowry advocated the acquisition of Sonora, probably because of his nearby investment property, by

---

36. "Colonization Decree of Sonora", May 6, 1850, ibid. The text of this Sonoran colonization decree is in the decree of the national congress that judged it unconstitutional, on the grounds that it asserted state powers reserved for the national government. See Patricia R. Herring, "A Plan for the Colonization of Sonora's Northern Frontier: The Paredes Proyectos of 1850," *Journal of Arizona History* 10 (Summer 1969): 103-14; Odie B. Faulk, trans. and ed., "Projected Mexican Military Colonies for the Borderlands, 1848," ibid. 9 (Spring 1968): 39-47; and Odie B. Faulk, trans. and ed., "Projected Mexican Colonies in the Borderlands, 1852," ibid. 10 (Summer 1969): 115-28.
37. *New York Times,* December 22, 24, 1852, and January 10, 1853.
38. La Gorce, *Histoire du second empire,* IV, 14. In 1857, the French government sent scientific teams to Mexico; Désiré Charnay, *Les anciennes villes du Nouveau Monde: voyages d'exploration au Mexique et dans L'Amerique Centrale, 1857-1882* (Paris, 1885), pp. 1, 152.

encouraging American emigration there. He asserted that Sonora's mineral wealth would equal or surpass that of the richest area in the world if it only had peace, capital, and a liberal government.[39]

In addition to Sylvester Mowry's enthusiastic appraisal, Captain Jim Box, a Texas ranger, accumulated mineral and agricultural data on the north Mexican states, while dismissing possible European protest over the balance of power principle if the United States were to acquire this area.[40] He descriptively insisted that the potential of Sonora's mines was sufficiently great to overcome any inconveniences. East of Arispe, a surface gold vein was visible more than three leagues away, while a silver mine nearby promised easy and rich profits. Box's article, virtually a miner's guidebook, contained page after page of detailed and colorful revelations of unexplored riches, silver mines that "run up for a mile," and gold that "exists upon all hands."[41] Six

---

39. The French scientist Malte-Brun, who wrote *La Sonora et ses mines,* referred to this address. Mowry, a West Point graduate and an officer at Fort Yuma in 1855, was elected as a delegate to Congress from the territory of Arizona. By 1860 he obtained the Patagonia Mine ten miles from the boundary line between Sonora and Arizona. He also had a particular interest in the port of Guaymas. Mowry, *Arizona and Sonora,* pp. 35, 48, 174-75, 235, 237.

40. Box, "Mines of Northern Mexico," 577. This article, writen to entice United States colonists to northern Mexico by "revelations of its almost illimitable riches," was published four months before the Tripartite Convention for European intervention in Mexico. It was based on the 1856 United States Boundary Commission report and on data subsequently collected by Captain Jim Box. Other extravagant claims, citing Mexican mining records, claimed that "the annual produce of a single silver mine exceeds a million of dollars." *Report of Frederick Brunckow to a Committee of the Stockholders of the Sonora Exploring and Mining Co. upon the History, Resources, and Prospects of the Company in Arizona* (Cincinnati: Railroad Record, 1859), p. 34.

41. Box, "Mines of Northern Mexico," 578-86. Writers from the United States concentrated on the gold mines of Sonora, while those from Europe emphasized the silver potential. See Bancroft, *North Mexican States,* I, 667-68, for gold discoveries in the 1770s in Sonora. Although von Humboldt generally depreciated Mexican gold, he emphasized that Sonora's gold "may be considered as the Choco of North America." Von Humboldt, *Essai politique,* III, 346-47. Also see Charles de Lambertie, *Le drame de Sonora* (Paris: Ledoyen, 1855); Alfred de Lachapelle, *Le comte de Raousset-Boulbon et l'expédition de la Sonore* (Paris: E. Dentu, 1859), pp. 74 ff.; and Carl Sartorius, *Mexico About 1850* (Stuttgart: F.A. Brockhaus Komm.-Gesch. G.M.B.H., Abt. Antiquarium, 1961), pp. 191-202, a reprint of the Darmstadt, 1858, edition. Maximilian had a personal copy of Sartorius, *Mexiko und die Mexikaner* (Darmstadt, 1852).

months before the article's publication, Benito Juárez had entered Mexico City, causing Box to believe that with the liberals in power emigrants would flock to Sonora, the "most auriferous portion of our continent."[42]

Such articles emanating from the United States nudged most European statesmen into the camp of conservative Mexicans. On January 19, 1862 Lord Palmerston, the British prime minister who had derisively scorned Mexico's disorders, wrote that if Mexico "could be turned into a prosperous Monarchy I do not know of any arrangement that would be more advantageous for us." And while Maximilian was en route to Mexico, some British journals reflected Palmerston's views and, quoting von Humboldt, Ward, and Michel Chevalier, they lauded the prospective changes for Mexico: with European techniques, the annual Mexican silver production could perhaps be tripled, and the unexplored mineral resources of Sonora, referred to as Mexico's richest mining district, would be developed.[43]

The French scientist Victor Adolphe Malte-Brun concurred that Sonora was undeniably one of the richest areas of the world in silver. Asserting that nowhere was there such "extraordinary" mineral potential, equal to the placers of both California and Australia, he echoed evaluations of Sonora's rich veins of "virgin silver" that was acquired in "slabs." Ironically, in the same year that Malte-Brun published his

---

42. Box, "Mines of Northern Mexico," 587. This belief was probably stimulated by Juárez's acceptance of the December 1859, McLane-Ocampo treaty which made many concessions to the United States. Although the United States Senate rejected it, Mexican conservatives alleged that national territory had been sold, while the liberals viewed the treaty as an extension of the 1831 and 1853 treaties. Bancroft, *History of Mexico,* V, 767-77. Mowry also believed that the prospects of Sonora greatly improved after 1859. Mowry, *Arizona and Sonora,* p. 92.

43. Assertions were made that the mines of Sonora and Lower California needed either a Mexican fleet or "the assistance of a naval squadron from France" to avoid their conquest by the United States. Robert Hogarth Patterson, "The Napoleonic Idea in Mexico," *Blackwood's Edinburgh Magazine* 96 (July 1864): 81. Palmerston to Russell, January 19, 1862, Harold Temperly and Lillian M. Penson, eds., *Foundations of British Foreign Policy: From Pitt (1792) to Salisbury (1902)* (London: Frank Cass, 1966), p. 295; and "Empire of Mexico," 349, 356, 364-65.

booklet, the Scientific Commission of Pachuca lamented "the exaggerated descriptions of Mexico that circulate throughout all of Europe."[44]

Malte-Brun estimated the annual mineral production in Sonora to be 5,082,500 francs, a figure more than three times the amount of silver francs coined in 1863.[45] Estimating the population of Sonora to be negligible, only one quarter white, Malte-Brun pointedly noted that the principal Indian tribes were docile Yaquis and Mayos who provided necessary agricultural and mining labor. Although he lightly touched on the dangerous Pimas and Seris, the French scientist treated the "perfidious" ten or twelve thousand Apaches more circumspectly, as they had unfortunately acquired firearms from the United States, contrary to Ward's report that they had only arrows. However, Malte-Brun seemed encouraged by Sylvester Mowry's interesting statement that the Apaches were not a serious obstacle to miners.[46]

---

44. Malte-Brun had founded the journal *Les nouvelles annales des voyages*. *La Sonora et ses mines* was published in booklet form in 1864 after its inclusion as an article in his journal the previous year. Victor Adolphe Malte-Brun, *La Sonora et ses mines* (Paris: Arthus Bertrand, 1864), pp. 5, 10-11, 22. References to Sonora as the "richest area of the world" are common in this period. See Lambertie, *Le drame de Sonora*, p. 10. Nearly seventy years after Malte-Brun's assessment, mining investors claimed that one-third of the several thousand operating Mexican mines were in Sonora, and that one of the largest lead-silver-zinc mines on the continent could be developed in northern Sonora. E. F. Schramm, *Report on Artemisa Mines Ltd. Located in Sonora, Mexico, with a Description of the Ore Deposits* (Bisbee, Arizona: Stockholders Report to President Oliver Kendall, Artemisa Mines, Ltd., 1932), pp. 6, 14; and *Comision Científica de Pachuca, 1864* (México: J. M. Andrade y F. Escalante, 1865), p. 6. Others asserted that Sonoran silver could have "speedily" eliminated the national debt of France. "The Plot of the Mexican Drama," *Eclectic* 6 (November 1867): 533.

45. Or 1,016,500 pesos, with 5 francs to the peso. This was considerably lower than the average annual mineral production of 7,500,000 francs from 1835 to 1850, a figure that still exceeded the total silver francs coined in France in 1864, when silver coinage accelerated. However, Stone's estimation of three to five million pesos, based on his 1858-59 surveys, was substantially higher than Malte-Brun's. Stone, "Sonora," 169. Adding agricultural and animal items, Malte-Brun estimated Sonora's annual productivity to be 2,708,000 pesos or 13,540,000 francs. Malte-Brun, *La Sonora*, pp. 17, 26. For French coinage figures, see Great Britain, *Hansard's Parliamentary Papers*, 3rd ser. (House of Commons), *Report on the Depreciation of the Price of Silver with Evidence and Papers from Representatives Abroad. Monetary Policy: Currency,* vol. 6. 1876 (Hereinafter cited as *Hansard's: Currency*), appendix, pp. 88-89.

46. Malte-Brun, *La Sonora*, pp. 3-6, 13-16; and Mowry, *Arizona and Sonora*, p. 68.

Sonora's mineral wealth, especially the *plaques d'argent* of the Arizona mine that enticed two French counts to their deaths in the 1850s, greatly interested the French scientist.[47] The inevitable perplexity of why so much wealth in Sonora had not been mined by impecunious Mexican governments was rather cursorily dismissed by Malte-Brun, Ward, and others by blaming neglect of the mines on political instability. Malte-Brun also derided efforts of mining adventurers who had sporadically tried to resuscitate Sonoran mines, commenting that they worked "without order and method." Citing statistics from *Travaux apostoliques de la Société de Jésus*, the French scientist stated that the Arizona mine had produced pieces of silver weighing one or two arrobas, and that one piece of silver from this mine had weighed 140 arrobas, or 3,550 pounds. He asserted, however, that the Arizona mine was merely representative, and that it would require a huge volume to describe all of the mines in detail, according to an "excellent" contemporary article on Sonora in the *Bulletin de la Société de Géographie de Genève,* which reinforced his contentions.[48] Malte-Brun, as others, believed modern metallurgy and scientific innovations would significantly increase Sonora's mineral production, and "immense profits" could be made if transportation, security, and good management were provided.[49] For the future, he

---

47. Malte-Brun, *La Sonora,* p. 22. One hundred years later, in 1964, much wrought silver was found in a shaft of this group of mines by Wayne Winters, an American mining engineer. Lately Thomas, *Between Two Empires: The Life Story of California's First Senator, William McKendree Gwin* (Boston: Houghton Mifflin, 1969), p. 291.

48. Malte-Brun, *La Sonora,* pp. 22-25. This was also the opinion of Saint-Clair-Duport, *De la production des métaux précieux au Mexique, considérée dans ses rapports avec la géologie, la métallurgie et l'économie politique* (Paris: F. Didot fréres, 1843), pp. 391-93. Also see Bancroft, *North Mexican States,* I, 527-28, on the Arizona mine.

49. Malte-Brun, *La Sonora,* pp. 26, 28. This, again, is also the contention of von Humboldt and many other writers. See Patterson, "The Napoleonic Idea in Mexico," 82; Stone, "Sonora," 169, who estimated mineral production could be increased "at least ten times"; and Mowry, *Arizona and Sonora,* pp. 123, 133-35. The French had given considerable attention to perfecting mining machinery and they displayed many new items at the Paris Universal Exposition of 1867. *House Ex. Doc.,* 41st Cong., 2nd sess., vol. 10, doc. 207, ser. 1424, "Mines and Mining," pp. 525, 591 ff.

suggested that a railroad be built to connect Guaymas, Hermosillo, Ures, and Arispe for maximum production and efficiency.[50]

Malte-Brun concluded with an eighteenth-century report to the viceroy of New Spain that predicted colonists in Sonora could produce mineral wealth that would astonish the world. Reminding Frenchmen that Spain had failed to develop these mines adequately, the scientist rhetorically challenged, "Which will be the nation that will fulfill this prediction?"[51] The answer was provided by Napoleon III. "With a boldness which pays little regard to what ordinary men call impossibilities," he sent Frenchmen to Mexico, a country three times the size of France.[52] From many sources the emperor had become convinced of the wealth of Sonora and the vulnerability of Mexico, and in 1861 he had a particularly acute need for silver.

50. Malte-Brun, *La Sonora,* p. 28. Also see Mowry, *Arizona and Sonora,* p. 93; for the Sonoran mines worked by Frenchmen in the 1850s, see Box, "Mines of Northern Mexico," 580.
51. Malte-Brun, *La Sonora,* pp. 28-29. Sylvester Mowry possessed a copy of a 1757 map, obtained by C. P. Stone, supposedly from the original in the Mexican archives. Mowry, *Arizona and Sonora,* p. 17. Also see article entitled "Sonora—Its Immense Wealth," *Mexican Times,* October 21, 1865, and October 15, 1866.
52. Patterson, "The Napoleonic Idea in Mexico," 72.

Chapter Three

The Bimetallic Crisis
in France

———•———

Although the Second French Empire is generally acknowledged to have been a period of prosperity, with the most rapid economic growth during the entire nineteenth century occurring in the decade after the coup d'état of 1851, Napoleon III faced a monetary crisis which motivated his enigmatic foreign policy toward Mexico. At the root of his problems was gold. In the twenty-five years between 1850 and 1875, the first twenty years coinciding with the Second Republic and Second Empire, the world's gold production equalled that of the previous 356 years, from 1493 to 1849.[1]

The influx of gold from Siberia, California, and Australia upset France's traditional bimetallic monetary system, causing, between 1853 and 1865, a revolution in the French currency. Silver, increasing in comparative value throughout the 1850s as gold production soared, was hoarded, melted down, and exported. The French need for silver intensified during the cotton crisis of the 1860s. As 93 percent of France's imports of raw cotton had come from the American South, its cotton industry suffered grievously when the Civil War curtailed this supply.[2]

---

1. Rondo Cameron et al., *Banking in the Early Stages of Industrialization: A Study in Comparative Economic History* (New York: Oxford University Press, 1967), p. 107; Adolf Soetbeer, *Edelmetall Produktion and werthverhältniss zwischen gold and silber, seit der entedeckung Amerika's bis zur gegenwart* (Gotha: J. Perthes, 1879), pp. 107-11; Alexander Del Mar, *A History of the Precious Metals: From the Earliest Times to the Present* (London: Geo. Bell & Sons, 1880), p. 447; J. E. Cairnes, *Essays in Political Economy* (London: Macmillan, 1873), pp. 115-16; and J. Laurence Laughlin, The *History of Bimetallism in the United States* (New York: D. Appleton, 1892), pp. 115-16.

2. Laughlin, *Bimetallism*, p. 119; Claude Fohlen, *L'industrie textile au temps du Second Empire* (Paris: Plon, [1956]), p. 128; and Frank Lawrence Owsley, *King Cotton Diplomacy: Foreign Relations of the Confederate States of America*, 2nd ed. rev. (Chicago: University of Chicago Press, 1959), pp. 14-15.

Napoleon's early efforts to solve the silver problem accelerated when alternate cotton suppliers in India demanded payment in silver.

The mines of Mexico, coveted earlier by the emperor's uncle, Napoleon Bonaparte, offered an obvious answer to the mounting economic problems of France.[3] Thus Napoleon III turned to Mexico as a source of that precious metal which would provide both the stabilization of the traditional French monetary standard and the medium to purchase raw cotton from India.

• • •

While economists later claimed that the emperor could have solved one of these pressing problems by adopting the gold standard, the massive influx of gold in the 1850s had no precedent, and his advisors conservatively urged him to retain the bimetallic standard. Great Britain was the only European country that had adopted, in 1816, a monometallic system, based on gold, before this avalanche began.[4] For centuries, the monetary policies of France had reflected a traditional reliance on silver.

Throughout the eighteenth century, while the English and Spanish mints favored gold, French currency was almost entirely silver.[5] Temporary aberrations had occurred, but the retention of a silver standard, in spite of enormous short-run difficulties, had been vindicated by later shifts in mineral productivity. During the twenty years between 1740 and 1760, Brazilian mines added an estimated £40 million to the world's stock of gold, activating Gresham's law that cheap money drives dearer money out of circulation. The shortage of silver currency became so great in 1759 that the French monarch and numbers of private individuals sent their plate to the mint.[6] However, after 1780 production of Mexican silver increased immensely. In 1785 Calonne, comptroller general of the finances under Louis XVI, implemented a recoinage that established gold at fifteen and a half times the value of silver (a ratio of 15.5:1), a policy that five years later, in 1790, the National Assembly severely

3. Lefebvre, *Napoleon*, I, 232-37.
4. André Piettre, *Monnaie et économie internationale du XIXe siècle à nos jours* (Paris: Editions Cujas, [1967]), p. 58.
5. Henri Sée, *Histoire économique de la France: Le moyen âge et l'ancien régime* (Paris: Librairie Armand Colin, 1948), pp. xx, 97, 166-71.
6. J. H. Clapham, *The Economic Development of France and Germany, 1815-1914*, 4th ed. (Cambridge: University Press, 1961), p. 376; Del Mar, *Precious Metals*, p. 255; and W. A. Shaw, *The History of Currency: 1252 to 1896*, 2nd ed. (London: Wilsons & Milne, 1896), p. 169.

moderated.[7] During the Consulate the monetary problem demanded a major amount of Napoleon Bonaparte's attention. Hoarded metallic currency caused a great scarcity of coin, and he tried to acquire silver and gold by increasing French exports and by "simple conquest." Turning to monetary methods of the *Ancien Régime,* by the Act of 7/17 *germinal, An* XI (March 20, 1803), Bonaparte reenacted Calonne's edict of 1785.[8] With knowledge of these previous monetary problems, Napoleon III presumed that the gold productivity of the 1850s was a bizarre episode which would stabilize without a major change in the French system.

According to the law of 1803, which remained in effect for seventy years, the silver franc was declared to be the monetary unit of France. At that time the mint ratio of 15.5:1 was nearly in accord with the relative market value of silver and gold. Although gold coins were also struck, enabling both metals to be accepted as legal tender, the circulating medium was almost exclusively silver.[9] However, from 1820 to

---

7. Laughlin, Bimetallism, p. 151; Sée, *Histoire économique,* pp. 170, 401; and Del Mar, *Precious Metals,* p. 180.

8. Lefebvre, *Napoleon,* I, 166-67; André Piettre, *Histoire économique: essai de synthèse faits et idées* (Paris: Editions Cujas, 1969), pp. 96-101; and for a concise résumé Horace White, "Bimetallism in France," *Political Science Quarterly* 6 (June 1891): 313-17. See Piettre, *Monnaie,* pp. 35-37, for the differences between the laws of 1785 and 1803, and Cameron, *Banking,* p. 102, for the concurrent changes in the Bank of France.

9. New discoveries of silver in Nevada and Colorado created a second monetary crisis in 1873. Piettre, *Monnaie,* pp. 35-36, 59; André Dargens and Fernand J. Tomiche, *L'or et son avenir* ([Paris]: Librairie Hachette, 1967), p. 63; Soetbeer, *Edelmetall-Produktion,* pp 130-32; Laughlin, *Bimetallism,* p. 119; Shaw, *Currency,* p. 176; and Henry Parker Willis, *A History of the Latin Monetary Union: A Study of International Monetary Action* (Chicago: University of Chicago Press, 1901), p. 8. There was much debate, primarily during the monetary emotionalism in the 1890s, on whether or not a bimetallic system was pragmatically possible. The intricate discussion on this point is not germane to this study. Although Horace White states, "When people talk to me about the double standard I say there is no such thing," he admits that "The only time after the passage of the law of 1803 when a dispute could have arisen touching the legal tender faculty of gold would have been the brief period (about 15 years) when the influx of gold from California and Australia had depressed the market ratio somewhat below 15.5." White, "Bimetallism" 329, 336. Also see H. Parker Willis, "The Operation of Bimetallism in France," *Journal of Political Economy 3* (June 1895): 356-62; and H. W. Stuart, "A Scarcity of Gold?" *Journal of Political Economy* 3 (June 1895): 362-65. However, Piettre refers to the French monetary system of this period as either "le système bimétalliste" or "le principe du double étalon".

1851, until the American and Australian gold entered Europe, gold was more valuable in the market than at the French mint. As a result of its scarcity, it was hoarded and exported, while large amounts of silver poured into France. Comparatively little gold was coined during this period, and in 1848 only one million francs of the fifty-three millions possessed by the Bank of France was in gold. Then, in 1851, the extraordinary production of gold resulted in a complete reversal. Gold deluged France, and silver, now more valuable in the market than at the French mint, became the metal that was hoarded and exported.[10]

Although it was estimated in the 1840s that France possessed one-third, or even more, of all money metals in Europe, Napoleon began his presidency of the Second French Republic in 1848 with a foretaste of the perplexities that the late gold discoveries would produce on the French monetary system. In 1840, while Louis Napoleon was failing in his second attempt to overthrow Louis Philippe, miners were succeeding in their efforts to extract gold from the tundra of Siberia. By 1847 France began to feel the effects of this new gold from Russia. Negligible in comparison to the subsequent Placerville and Bendigo discoveries, the output from these alluvial deposits in the Urals and Siberia increased almost four-fold from 1840 to 1847 and permeated throughout Europe.[11]

• • •

During the first decade that Napoleon III was in power, the French coinage system completely reversed. Before 1851 gold formed less than one fourth of the coinage, while more than three-fourths

10. Michel Chevalier, *De la baisse probable de l'or, des conséquences commerciales et sociales qu'elle peut avoir et des mesures qu'elle provoque* (Paris: Capelle, 1859), p. 215; *Rapport de la commission chargée d'étudier la question de l'étalon monétaire* (Paris: Ministère des finances, 1869), p. 32; White, "Bimetallism," 333; and *Enquête sur les principes et les faits généraux qui régissent la circulation monétaire et fiduciaire*, 6 vols. (Paris: Conseil supérieur de l'agriculture, du commerce, et de l'industrie, 1869), VI, 534-35. See also Alain Plessis "La révolution métallique" in *La Politique de la Banque de France de 1851-1870* (Genève: Droz,1985), pp. 118-27.

11. The estimation of one-third was made by Léon Faucher who had close business connections with Baron James de Rothschild. Cameron, *Banking*, p. 117; Willis, *Monetary Union*, p. 18; Del Mar, *Precious Metals*, p. 389; Cairnes, *Political Economy*, p. 115; R. G. Hawtrey, *The Gold Standard in Theory and Practice*, 5th ed. (London: Longmans, Green, 1947), p. 47; and Clapham, *Economic Development*, p. 376.

was silver. In the ensuring ten years, however, the coinage ratio inverted, and more than three-fourths of the coinage was gold, while less than one-fourth was silver.[12]

This disturbance in the relative production of silver and gold, resulting in a rapid coinage transition, created a startling revolution in French monetary habits.[13] Uncertainty about how to resolve the crisis of the complete change in France's stock of coins led in the early 1850s, to a special government commission, headed by Adolphe Thiers, to study the monetary situation. By 1852, for the first time since the Restoration, exports of silver actually exceeded imports. This imbalance continued through 1864, the year that Maximilian became emperor of Mexico.[14]

While French economists and financiers struggled with severe monetary problems, the drain of silver continued. The average annual export of silver increased over seven fold, from 31.3 million francs per year between 1815 and 1847 to 226.8 millions per year from 1848 until 1861, the year France signed the Tripartite Convention with England and Spain to intervene in Mexico.[15]

This loss of silver drastically changed French coinage. In 1854 the

---

12. "Relevé par année des espèces d'or et d'argent fabriquées en France", enclosures 2 and 3 from Decazes to Lyons, April 10, 1876, *Hansard's: Currency*, appendix, pp. 88-89; and Emile Levasseur, *La question de l'or* (Paris: Guillaumin et cie, 1858), p. 105. England, too, was undergoing a monetary problem in 1857. J. R. McCulloch, *A Select Collection of Scarce and Valuable Tracts and Other Publications, on Paper Currency and Banking* (London: 1857), p. xviii; and Sir Albert Feavearyear, *The Pound Sterling: A History of English Money*, 2nd ed. rev. (Oxford: Clarendon Press, 1963), p. 292 ff.

13. Willis, *Monetary Union*, p. 1. Although an evaluation of prices is superfluous to this study, prices increased after the gold discoveries. Laughlin, *Bimetallism*, p. 38 ff. Analyses of statistics, causes, and results vary. A summary of the conclusions of the German economists, Sauerbeck, Soetbeer, and Kral, is in Stuart, "Gold," 362-65; and a comparative analysis of the French economists Gustave Cassel, Charles Rist, and Robert Marjolin is in Piettre, *Monnaie*, pp. 70-71.

14. *Documents relatifs à la question monétaire, Procès-verbaux et rapport de la commission monétaire de 1867 relatifs à la question de l'étalon* (Paris, 1868), p. 6; and *Enquête sur les principes et les faits généraux quir régissent la circulation monétaire et fiduciaire*, 1869, VI, 534-35. For the relationship between the monetary circulation and the financial and commercial panic of 1857, see Clément Juglar, *Des crises commerciales et de leur retour périodique en France, en Angleterre et aux Etats-Unis*, 2nd ed. (Paris: 1889). For the situation in 1864, see H. Bordet, *L'Or et L'Argent en 1864* (Paris, Guillaumin, 1864).

15. *Enquete sur le circulation monétaire et fiduciaire*, VI (1869), 534-35; and *Hansard's: Currency*, appendix, pp. 86-87.

mint produced only 2,123,887 francs in silver, the smallest amount coined since 1795.[16] By 1855 the lack of silver caused great consternation and active discussion about the resultant problems and possible solutions. In 1860, a year before the French intervened in Mexico, fiscal experts deemed the monetary question in France "an imperious dilemma."[17]

There were three alternatives for the French: (1) to retain the status quo, permitting the law of 1803 to continue; (2) to demonetize silver; (3) to demonetize gold. For a variety of reasons, including tradition and the belief that this would provide greater stability, the French government chose the first alternative and attempted to maintain a bimetallic standard. Adamant about maintaining a specie standard, monetary authorities were reluctant to introduce a new system in France for fear of making a mistake in the selection of the metal to be demonetized. Arguing that the traditional monetary policy had rendered great service, they predicted that it would continue to meet future commercial needs.[18]

---

16. From 1848 to 1867, France alone coined 40 percent of the total world production of gold. Cameron, *Banking*, p. 117. The figures quoted for French coinage include only the coinage for France. *Hansard's: Currency*, appendix, p. 89. Nine years later, in 1863, the year that the French marched into Mexico City, French silver coinage hit an astonishing low of merely 329,610 francs.

17. Henri Baudrillart, "Des crises monétaires et de la question de l'or," *Journal des économistes*, 2nd ser., 7 (July-September 1855): 360-89; E. de Pariu, "La question monétaire française," *Journal des économistes*, 2nd ser., 26 (April-June 1860): 1; and *Rapport de la commission chargée d'étudier la question monétaire. Documents relatifs à la question monétaire* (Paris: Ministère des Finances, Enquête de 1858), p. 8.

18. Piettre, *Monnaie*, p. 36; Philip S. Bagwell and G. E. Mingay, *Britain and America, 1850-1939: A Study of Economic Change* (London: Routledge & Kegan Paul, 1970), p. 137; and Cameron, *Banking*, p. 117. This continued into the twentieth century, as the French economist Charles Rist scathingly condemned Lord Keynes' lack of respect for specie. Charles Rist, *The Triumph of Gold*, trans. Philip Cortney from the French ed., *La défense de l'or* (New York: Philosophical Library, 1961), p. 191; R. de Fontenay, "La question monétaire," *Journal des économistes*, 2nd ser., 26 (April-June 1860): 398 et seq.; Parieu, "La question monétaire française," *Journal des économistes*, 2nd ser., 26 (April-June 1860): 2 ff.; *Rapport de la commission chargée d'étudier la question monétaire*, 1858, pp. 39 ff.; and *Conférence monétaire internationale entre la Belgique, la France, l'Italie, et la Suisse, Procès-verbaux, 1865*, Séance I, pp. 22-23, cited by Willis, *Monetary Union*, p. 45.

The Bank of France was an important defender of the monetary standard established in 1803; and, for both political and military reasons, there was necessarily a strong entente cordiale between Napoleon III and the national bank.[19] By mid century bankers were working diligently to meet the new demands for capital necessitated by extraordinary economic activity. For the only time from the Restoration to the end of the nineteenth century, the metallic reserve in the bank decreased considerably, over 178 million francs from 1852 to 1861. Trying to retain specie reserves as a guarantee of note liabilities, the bank desperately and publicly offered a premium for silver bullion over the mint ratio.[20] In spite of these difficulties M. Rouland, governor of the Bank of France, insisted that both gold and silver were still necessary in the nation's monetary circulation. The bank's regents supported him. Baron James (also called Jacob) de Rothschild queried, "How would it be possible to demonetize a sum of 15 or 16 hundred millions of silver. . . . Could one find gold to fill the vacancy?"[21] As the government of Napoleon III labored with the violent change in the monetary system, the bank exerted conspicuous influence on commissions and decisions. In consultations between the French finance minister and bank officers, the

19. A. Soetbeer, *Materialien zur Erklärung und Beurtheilung der wirth-schaftlichen Edelmetallverhältnisse und der währungsfrage*, p. 29, cited by Willis, *Monetary Union*, p. 58; and Laughlin, *Bimetallism*, p. 148. Also see *Correspondance de Napoléon Ier, publiée par l'ordre de l'Empéreur Napoléon III*, 32 vols. (Paris, 1858-70), XVII, 497-500, on the Bank of France, reprinted in S. Pollard and C. Holmes, eds., *Documents of European Economic History* ([London]: Edward Arnold, [1968]), vol. 1, *The Process of Industrialization, 1750-1870*, pp. 455-56.

20. Rondo Cameron, *France and the Economic Development of Europe, 1800-1914: Conquests of Peace and Seeds of War* (Princeton: Princeton University Press, 1961), pp. 119, 526; and White, "Bimetallism," 334. As the specie reserves of the Bank of France rarely fell below 80 percent of its note liabilities, the bank itself was the greatest "hoarder" of metal. See particularly Roger Price, *An Economic History of Modern France 1730-1914*, rev. ed. (Macmillan, London, 1981) pp. 154-59.

21. *Enquête sur la question monétaire Décembre 1869-Août 1871* (Paris: Conseil supérieur de l'agriculture, du commerce, et de l'industrie, 1872), pp. 68, 110-11, 124.

bank's recommendations were uniformly followed, further activating animated debates.22

The scarcity of small silver coin, not the selection of a particular monetary standard, stimulated demands for government action. As silver was indispensable for daily transactions, its disappearance had a paralyzing effect on the economy. In 1858 a commission, one of many appointed to resolve the predicament, summarized the major problems: (1) the most important disadvantage to the treasury was the considerable expense of buying silver for additional coinage; (2) a reserve composed of gold instead of silver constituted a danger to the bank, as the greater portability of gold caused easier withdrawals that might result in serious fluctuations in the bank's reserve and in the rate of discount; and (3) the disappearance of silver caused commercial difficulties because of the necessity of buying silver ingots at a premium for use in trade with the East. The commission ineffectively recommended that a high tariff be placed upon the export of silver and that money speculators be rigidly controlled. This failed to solve the problem which required much more extreme action.23 Immense amounts of silver were necessary to maintain either a silver or a bimetallic standard preferred by influential French economists and financiers.

Both Belgium, whose King Leopold was Maximilian's father-in law,

---

22. Henri Baudrillart, "Chronique économique," *Journal des économistes*, 2nd ser., 12 (October-December 1856): 474 ff.; and Willis, *Monetary Union*, p. 58. During the 1848 crisis the bank, with government authorization, became the sole source of paper currency. After the establishment of the Second Empire, however, the bank's "stranglehold" on some aspects of the French financial system was temporarily broken. Cameron, *Banking*, pp. 104-05, 109, 127; See Levasseur, *La question de l'or*, supportive of a gold standard; Chevalier, *De la baisse probable de l'or*, favorable to a silver standard; and L. F. M. R. Wolowski, *L'or et l'argent* (Paris: Guillaumin et cie, 1870), for continuation of bimetallism. For a penetrating analysis of French banking and major bankers, see Guy P. Palmade, *French Capitalism in the Nineteenth Century* (New York, Barnes & Noble, 1972), pp. 105-48; and D. Landes, "The Old Bank and the New: The Financial Revolution of the Nineteenth Century" in F. Crouzet, W.H. Chaloner and W.M. Stern, eds., *Essays in European Economic History 1789-1914* (New York, St. Martins, 1969), pp. 112-27.

23. *Rapport de la commission chargée d'étudier la question monétaire*, 1858, pp. 23-28; Hawtrey, *Gold Standard*, p. 65; and *Enquête sur la question monétaire*, 1872, I, 12-13.

and Switzerland, the homeland of Jean Baptiste Jecker, were periph-
erally involved in the Mexican intervention; both of these countries
had monetary crises similar to, and sometimes exceeding, those of
France. In 1832, after acquiring independence from Holland,
Belgium had adopted the French coinage system.[24] Due to geo-
graphic position, conflicting monetary standards staggered Belgium,
placed between France, with its dilemma, England, "where gold is in
law and fact the sole standard, Holland where silver is in law and fact
also the sole monetary metal, and Germany where silver is the sole
legal standard, but where gold nevertheless obtains a very important
effective circulation."[25]

For Belgium the lack of silver created agonizing hardships, as well as
bitterness toward France. From 1854, when Belgian silver coinage
ceased, to 1865, Belgium relied totally on the French mint for silver, as
this was less costly than operating their own mint. In 1854, the year that
the Belgians first minted no silver, the French minted only 2,123,887
francs—as has been noted above, the lowest amount of silver coined
since 1795. Monetary problems mounted, as silver was hoarded and
exported by speculators who collected the newer, less worn coins.[26]

---

24. *Senate Reports,* 44th Cong., 2nd sess., *Report of the United States Monetary
   Commission,* 1876, vol. 5, pt. 1, ser. 1738, doc. 703, appendix, p. 144. From
   1847 to 1850, Belgium tried to operate independently of France by
   attempting to secure a gold currency. Holland demonetized gold in 1847
   and the Russian gold entering France that same year displaced silver. The
   subsequent reduction of French silver coinage forced Belgium, for three
   years, to rely on its own mint for subsidiary coin instead of on the French
   mint.

25. Speech delivered by M. Kreglinger at the opening session of the first convention of the Latin Monetary Union, December 23, 1865, cited by Willis,
   Monetary Union, p. 24.

26. From 1854 to 1865 no Belgian silver was coined except for the negligible
   total in 1858 of 263,560 francs: 90,510 five-franc pieces and 173,050 twenty centimes. *Hansard's: Currency,* appendix, pp. 86–91. See Hawtrey, *Gold
   Standard,* p. 80, on the high cost of coinage. The better part of the Belgian
   silver circulation was profitably exchanged for worn French coins, much of
   which had lost 8 percent of their value by wear. The heavier Belgian coin
   was then melted and exported to the two major silver standard countries,
   Holland and Germany. M. J. Malou, *Documents relatifs à la question monétaire* (Bruxelles, 1874), pp. 176–77; *Rapport déposé par M. le Ministre des
   Finances à la chambre des Représentants,* Séance du 20 Août, 1859, Question
   monétaire, no. 18.

Desperate for silver coins, Belgian imports of precious metals from France jumped from 6 million francs in 1850 to 78 million francs in 1859.[27] In spite of this, the monetary situation became still more critical. The increasing premium on silver caused even the worn coins to disappear, and the severely felt lack of an adequate currency constituted an emergency. During intense debate over what measures to take, the Belgian finance minister, H.J.W. Frère-Orban, resigned on June 4, 1861. Just the previous week, the French foreign minister had received a request for forces to be sent to silver-rich Mexico.[28]

Switzerland had monetary difficulties similar to France and Belgium. By the *Bundesverfassung* of 1848, coinage was placed under the control of the central government, and in May 1850 it instituted the French monetary system, as established by the law of 1803. Then French gold began to replace Swiss silver, and by 1855 silver coins were extremely scarce. Public discussion became spirited, and in 1859 the *Bundesrath* acknowledged the "urgency of circumstances." The fineness in silver coinage was decreased in January 1860, but these coins were imported into France and Belgium where they profitably displaced the old coins which were then melted and exported.[29] In spite of attempted solutions, Switzerland, like France and Belgium, continued to suffer from a great lack of silver currency.

The scarcity of coins and the reduced bank reserves were only one

---

27. Of the 78 millions, 76.3 were silver. Malou, *Question monétaire*, pp. 176-77.
28. The scarcity of small coins was a serious impediment to business and trade; the reserves of the *Banque Nationale* were depleted, first of gold and then of silver and sometimes of both; and the rate of discount fluctuated between the extreme limits of 3 and 6 percent from a normal rate of 2.5-3 percent. *Hansard's: Currency*, appendix, pp. 102-06. Saligny to Thouvenel, April 28, 1861. Thouvenel received Saligny's request on May 29, 1861. Carl H. Bock, *Prelude to Tragedy: The Negotiation and Breakdown of the Tripartite Convention of London, October 31, 1861* (Philadelphia: University of Pennsylvania Press, 1966), pp. 123, 642.
29. Willis, *Monetary Union*, p. 26; A. E. Cherbuliez, "La question monétaire en Suisse," *Journal des économistes*, 2nd ser., 25 (January March 1860): 40-42; J. E. Horn, "La crise monétaire," *Journal des économistes*, 2nd ser., 31 (July-September 1861): 11-12; and Laughlin, *Bimetallism*, pp. 147-60. From early 1860 to the end of 1863 a total of 10.5 million francs, in one-franc and two-franc pieces, were struck, the same in weight and appearance as the French and Belgian, although containing 10 percent less fine silver. *Hansard's: Currency*, appendix, pp. 102-06.

facet of the French need for silver. Textiles were France's most important industry, and the lack of cotton during the American Civil War caused serious repercussions. Although there was some speculation about the potential for Mexican cotton, France turned to India for rapid supplies. Indian suppliers, however, inconveniently demanded payment in silver.[30]

Napoleon acutely needed silver, as he now faced severe economic and employment problems as well as monetary distress. In addition to the impact of the American Civil War on the textile industry, the war virtually crippled the French export industry. Suffering first from the loss of the American market, the export trade reeled further as other European countries, similarly affected by decreased exports and, subsequently, by the lack of cotton, also bought less luxury goods. Even before "the American crisis" exploded in April 1861, France felt repercussions from the high protective Morrill tariff and from the heightening tensions between the North and the South which resulted in reductions of French exports.[31]

---

30. Robert Lévy, *Histoire économique de l'industrie cotonnière en Alsace: étude de sociologie descriptive* (Paris: Alcan, 1912), p. 168; and Louis Reybaud, *Le coton: son régime, ses problèms—son influence en Europe* (Paris: Michel Lévy frères, 1863), appendix, pp. 412-38. Raw cotton consumption, increasing five-fold from 1815-45, had expanded still more rapidly in the 1850s. Cameron, *Banking*, p. 113; Earl S. Pomeroy, "French Substitutes for American Cotton, 1861-1865," *Journal of Southern History* 9 (November 1943): 557; Owsley, *Cotton Diplomacy*, p. 529; Karl Ellstaetter, *The Indian Silver Currency: An Historical and Economic Study*, trans. J. Laurence Laughlin (Chicago: University of Chicago Press, 1895); and Piettre, *Monnaie*, p. 59.

31. For import-export statistics, see Henry Blumenthal, *A Reappraisal of Franco-American Relations, 1830-1871* (Chapel Hill: University of North Carolina Press, 1959), pp. 102-09; and *Historical Statistics of the United States, From Colonial Times to 1957* (Washington, D.C.: United States Government Printing Office, 1960), p. 553. French imports from America were primarily cotton and tobacco. Clément Juglar, *Des crises commerciales et de leur retour périodique en France, en Angleterre et aux Etats-Unis*, 2nd ed. (Paris: Guillaumin et cie, 1889), pp. 17, 279; and Lynn M. Case, *French Opinion on the United States and Mexico, 1860-1867: Extracts from the Reports of the Procureurs Généraux* (New York: D. Appleton-Century, 1936), pp. 10-45, 101, 109, 111, 121, 139; The Morrill tariff was introduced by the United States in 1861. J. E. Horn, "Bulletin financier de l'étranger," *Journal des économistes*, 2nd ser., 35 (July-September 1862): 325.

The lack of cotton had a widening impact on the French economy: as factories and related industries closed down, both the price of cotton goods and unemployment increased. The emperor was particularly concerned about unemployment. In an interview with Richard Cobden in 1859, Napoleon, expressing caution about commercial changes, stated, "Nous ne faisons pas de reformes en France; nous ne faisons que des revolutions."[32] Unfortunately, the Anglo-French Treaty of Commerce of January 1860 was implemented in October 1861, just when the effects of the cotton famine were being felt in France. Napoleon, like the Bourbons, hardly dared to oppose organized cotton manufacturers, and he urgently wanted to minimize the distress to this important industry.[33]

When the Northern blockade was proclaimed in April 1861, Henri Mercier, French ambassador to the United States, expressed grave concern about France's winter supply of raw cotton. Although a previous French surplus and the accelerated imports of American cotton from 1860 to the outbreak of the Civil War initially enabled most cotton manufacturers to continue operations, by the fall of

---

32. Although estimates on unemployment vary from 275,000 to 400,000, imperial censorship forbade the press to mention unemployment and industrial discontent. London *Times,* January 8 and 13, 1863. Also see Claude Fohlen, "Crise textile et troubles sociaux: le Nord à la fin du Second Empire," *Revue du Nord,* 1953:107-23; Fohlen, *L'industrie textile au temps du Second Empire,* pp. 161-249; Owsley, *Cotton Diplomacy,* p. 152; W. O. Henderson, *The Lancashire Cotton Famine, 1861-1865,* p. 196; and Cobden to Palmerston, October 29, 1859, *Cobden Papers,* cited by Arthur Louis Dunham, *The Anglo-French Treaty of Commerce of 1860 and the Progress of the Industrial Revolution in France* (Ann Arbor: University of Michigan Press, 1930), p. 58.

33. To give the French cotton industry time to prepare for British competition, and also because the French government, in 1856, promised not to remove prohibitions in the tariff for five years, the treaty's provisions on cotton did not take effect until October 1861, according to clause five of article sixteen. Ibid., pp. 192-93; Napoleon III to Fould, January 5, 1860, reprinted in Pollard and Holmes, eds., *Documents of European Economic History,* I, 384-86; Frank Arnold Haight, *A History of French Commercial Policies* (New York: Macmillan Company, 1941), p. 32. For text of the treaty, see either Dunham, *Anglo-French Treaty,* appendix, pp. 185, 369-71; or Pollard and Holmes, eds., *European Economic History,* I, 389-95. See also Piettre, *Monnaie,* pp. 105-09; and Reybaud, *Le coton,* p. 419.

1861 the government was besieged with complaints and petitions from commercial centers. Twenty-seven days before the Tripartite Convention authorizing intervention in Mexico, the French foreign minister, Edouard Thouvenel, expressed anxiety about France's cloth production, "worth 700 million francs," which was seriously endangered by the lack of "indispensable cotton." [34] The urgency for cotton demanded importation of raw materials from silver-consuming countries at the same time that the need for silver was becoming more acute. Within this context in 1861 France began taking more strident steps in Mexico, the world's major silver producer.

French economic and unemployment problems increased when both imports of cotton and cotton stock in warehouses fell alarmingly from 1861 to 1862. While scattered areas showed some resiliency, others were confronted with serious unemployment by the end of 1861. In eastern Normandy, over 40 percent of the workers involved in spinning and hand weaving in the important region of Rouen were unemployed. Export industries suffered similar distress. By the winter of 1861-62, 55 percent of clock and watch workers in the Rouen area were unemployed, while the Limoges china industry reduced production 50 percent.[35]

Frantically trying to find relief for these problems, the emperor, the foreign minister, and French bankers pressured Union diplomats.

---

34. Mercier to Thouvenel, Washington, May 6, 1861, cited by Lynn M. Case and Warren F. Spencer, *The United States and France: Civil War Diplomacy* (Philadelphia: University of Pennsylvania Press, 1970), p. 135; Figures for 1860 and 1861 are somewhat deceptive due to abnormally large American crops in 1859 and 1860 that were purchased in anticipation of a disturbance of supply from America. *London Economist*, November 2, 1861; M. B. Hammond, *The Cotton Industry*, (New York: Macmillan, 1897), p. 258; Dunham, *Anglo-French Treaty*, p. 194; Fohlen, *L'industrie textile*, pp. 284-86; Owsley, *Cotton Diplomacy*, 134-36; and Thouvenel to Mercier, Paris, October 3, 1861, cited by Case and Spencer, *United States and France*, pp. 170-71; also see October 1861 reports of the procureurs général, Case, *United States and Mexico*, pp. 17-26.

35. Imported cotton dropped form 624,600 bales in 1861 to 271,570 bales in 1862. Cotton stock decreased in the same period from 140,345 bales to 59,193 bales. Dunham, *Anglo-French Treaty*, p. 193. "Reports of the procureurs généraux", July and October 1861 and January 1862, reprinted in Case, *United States and Mexico*, pp. 13-45.

In March 1862, Napoleon urged William L. Dayton, United States minister to France, to do "something" to "relieve the difficulties here."[36] Thouvenel instructed Mercier about the serious manufacturing problems due to the lack of cotton, and he then sternly told Henry Sanford, United States minister in Brussels, "We are nearly out of cotton, and cotton we *must have*."[37] Baron James de Rothschild directly confronted Sanford, stating that the lack of American cotton had caused a "convulsion" in France, and ambiguously added, "When your patient is desperately sick, you try desperate remedies, even to blood-letting."[38] In Napoleon's July 1862 letter to General Elie Frédéric Forey, commander of French forces in Mexico, the emperor protested both United States domination of Latin America and the adverse effects on France of the United States' posture as "the sole distributor of the products of the New World."[39] Plagued by gold and cotton problems emanating from the United States, Napoleon was enraged by the dependency and helplessness of France.

From July to October 1862, the impact of the American Civil War on French cotton and export industries became more intense. The new foreign minister, Edouard Drouyn de Lhuys, who replaced Thouvenel in October 1862, lamented the "crisis which is preventing the growth of one of the most fertile sources of public wealth and which is becoming, for the great centers of labor, the cause of a most painful situation."[40] The last months of 1862 and the first half of 1863 were the most severe period of the cotton crisis. By 1862 the weekly average consumption of cotton dropped to about one-half of the 1861 amount, causing cotton prices to be often higher than wool and linen.

---

36. Dayton to Seward, Paris, March 25, 1862, cited by Case and Spencer, *United States and France,* p. 289.
37. Thouvenel to Mercier, March 13, 1862, cited by Ephraim Douglass Adams, *Great Britain and the American Civil War* (New York: Russell & Russell, 1958), p. 279; and Sanford to Seward, April 10, 1862 (rcd. April 25), cited by Case and Spencer, *United States and France,* p. 290.
38. Sanford to Seward, Paris, April 10, 1862 (rcd. April 25), ibid.
39. Kathryn Abbey Hanna, "Incidents of the Confederate Blockade," *Journal of Southern History* 11 (February 1945): 215.
40. "Economic reports of the procureurs généraux", July-October 1862, reprinted in Case, *United States and Mexico,* pp. 70-100; and Drouyn de Lhuys to French ambassadors in St. Petersburg and London, Paris, October 30, 1862, printed in *Le Moniteur Universel,* November 13, 1862.

By April 1863, the total number of unemployed Frenchmen was approximately 223,336, affecting the lives of an estimated 670,000 persons. Aware of potential unrest, the emperor instigated and accelerated public work projects to relieve unemployed workers. It was clear, however, that France urgently needed silver to purchase cotton from India. At this time of greatest unemployment, the French foreign minister ambiguously told the United States minister to France that Napoleon did not intend to take Sonora—permanently.[41]

Both England and France reluctantly turned to silver-standard India for cotton. Although French firms made substantial investments in Egypt, Algeria, West Africa, and Turkey before and during the cotton famine, India provided the major source of cotton.[42] However, a year's delay was necessary before the production of Indian cotton could be adequately increased, and raw cotton from India did not begin to arrive in France until 1862. Even when it did arrive, there were many problems: Indian cotton had a shorter staple, many impurities, and resulted in yarn that caused threads to break more easily. These complications forced cotton manufacturers into laborious and expensive adaptations of their machinery to Indian cotton. Although Michel Chevalier advocated, and the French government implemented, substantial loans to aid cotton manufacturers with this situation, the complicated change of machinery caused many small mills to go bankrupt.[43]

---

41. Fohlen, *L'industrie textile*, pp. 253-55, 265-67; and Dunham, *Anglo-French Treaty*, pp. 155-60, 198, 272. Weekly consumption of cotton dropped from 11,114 bales in 1861 to 5,981 bales in 1862. Average consumption then increased in 1863 to nearly 7,000 bales a week, and in 1864 French consumption of cotton was nearly 8,000 bales weekly, about three-fourths of the 1861 amount. Owsley, *King Cotton Diplomacy*, pp. 152-53; David H. Pinkney, *Napoleon III and the Rebuilding of Paris* (Princeton, N.J.: Princeton University Press, 1958), p. 37; and Dayton to Seward, Paris, April 24, 1863, excerpts reprinted in Case and Spencer, *United States and France*, pp. 519-20.

42. For the conflict between England and India over India's troublesome silver standard, see Hawtry, *Gold Standard*, pp. 77-78; Pomeroy, "French Substitutes for American Cotton," 557; and Dunham, *Anglo-French Treaty*, p. 166.

43. Although imports had increased from 271,570 bales in 1862 to 381,539 by the end of 1863, the total French stock fell from 59,193 bales in 1862 to 32,852 in 1863. Dunham, *Anglo-French Treaty*, pp. 153 ff., 193, 198-99, 201, 210; Owsley, *King Cotton Diplomacy*, p. 5, citing the *London Economist*, April 13, 1861; and Clapham, *Economic Development of France and Germany*, p. 246.

While Napoleon struggled with these monetary, manufacturing, and employment problems, French exports of silver continued. India, having demonetized gold in 1850, absorbed vast quantities of silver.[44] From 1852 through 1864 France exported over one and a half billion francs of silver, and the additional strain of a new cotton source worsened the government's position. In May 1864, the *corps législatif,* in response to popular outcry against the lack of specie, passed a law to reduce the amount of silver in the 50 and 20 centime coins. Contrary to expectations, this failed to rectify the silver shortage. As soon as small coins were minted, speculators absorbed them and, evading the new restrictive laws, continued their profitable manipulations. In the earlier part of 1865 Belgium, more severely affected than the other three countries due to its retention of the old silver fineness, proposed that a joint monetary conference be held. France, Switzerland, and Italy readily accepted the invitation, and the Latin Monetary Union was formed. France considered the lack of silver subsidiary coin the major issue, and it was this, not a change in the monetary standard, that was most heatedly debated.[45]

When French troops entered Mexico, that nation's silver, which had previously gone to Great Britain and the United States, started flowing into France. French imports of Mexican bullion and specie more than doubled from 1861 to 1862, and doubled again from 1862 to 1863. Even with greatly augmented silver supplies, France's need was so great that its monetary problems did not lessen significantly until 1865. In that year, for the first time since Napoleon III became emperor, France imported more silver than was exported.[46] Widely criticized for his policies in Mexico, he was supported by those who anticipated that the French would increase Mexican min-

44. *Enquête sur la circulation monétaire,* VI, 534-35; Ellstaetter, *Indian Silver Currency;* and Laughlin, *History of Bimetallism,* pp. 122-34, 218.
45. More specifically, 1,727 million francs, or over $345 million. *Enquête sur la circulation monétaire,* VI, 534-35; and Willis, *Monetary Union,* pp. 41, 43, 47.
46. *Hansard's: Currency,* appendix, pp. 86-87, 708. The British did not regain their predominance of Mexican silver shipments to Europe until the end of the Second Empire. The United States, whose receipt of Mexican metals was reduced more than one-half during the French intervention, regained its preferential status in 1867.

ing productivity, restore the balance between silver and gold, and stop the escalating price of silver.[47]

Mexico's wealth of silver and France's dearth of this metal coincided with a period of vulnerability for both countries. The implications of von Humboldt's work were that Sonora's mineral wealth could easily restore the world's balance between gold and silver,[48] and in the 1850s only two hundred Frenchmen, led by the adventurous Count Gaston Raoul de Raousset-Boulbon, were to prove how vulnerable Sonora really was.

47. "The Empire of Mexico," 361; and Patterson, "The Napoleonic Idea in Mexico," 72, 82. For silver prices, see "Ratio of Silver to Gold," computed monthly from 1845 to 1880 by O. J. Broch, "French Report on Conference of 1881," reprinted in Laughlin, *History of Bimetallism*, appendix 2, p. 225.
48. Mowry, *Arizona and Sonora*, p. 54. See La Gorce, *Second empire*, IV,14, for von Humboldt's influence on Napoleon III; also, *Journal de la société des Americanistes de Paris*, 10 vols. (Paris:1903-1913), X, 285-86.

Chapter Four

French Expeditions to Sonora
1851-1854

———•———

During the early 1850s, while Napoleon III was confronting both the Russians in the Crimean War and monetary problems at home, several Frenchmen led expeditions seeking Mexican mineral wealth. After the discovery of gold in California, it seemed logical that the same mountains rendering wealth there would not disappoint those who followed their southward extension into Mexico.

The reported wealth of silver in Sonora and the French need for this metal were complemented by Sonora's perilous position.[1] Mexico's borders receded drastically when the United States acquired about half of Mexico's national domain by the Treaty of Guadalupe Hidalgo, signed in Querétaro on February 2, 1848. Less than two weeks earlier, gold had been discovered in California, and adventurers rapidly descended on this area northwest of Sonora. For many, when dreams of wealth and power there soon evaporated, frustration and hope turned them toward the fabled wealth of northern Mexico.[2]

---

1. Sonora was one of the most isolated states of Mexico. Its major towns, developed from missions and presidios, were Ures, the capital; Hermosillo, the largest with a population in the 1850s of about 12,000; Arispe, military headquarters and former capital; Guaymas, the only important port; and Alamos, the mining center of southern Sonora

2. Bancroft, *North Mexican States,* II, 673-75, 720-21. The heading, "Expected Invaders from California," a warning from Manuel Brenas, prefect of Alamos, to José de Aguilar, governor of Sonora, April 9, 1851, is typical of the alarms in Sonora during this era. *El Sonorense,* May 30, September 5 and November 7, 1851, reprinted in Alphonse Pinart, *Documents for the History of Sonora: Extracts from Manuscripts and Printed Matter in the Collection of Mons. Alphonse Pinart* (MSS, Bancroft Library, University of California, Berkeley, California, Mexican MSS, nos. 286-92), V, 312, 334, 342. The Pinart Collection will be cited hereinafter as *Pinart Transcripts, Sonora.*

In the 1850s, Sonora resembled California in the 1840s: both had mineral wealth, factional governments, and lack of protection from a distant central government. Since California had changed from a province of Mexico to a possession of the United States within only five years after the arrival of the first group of settlers from the United States, officials in Sonora were justifiably apprehensive.[3]

Almost at once several modest attempts to invade Sonora materialized, none involving more than 300 men. Many were simply bands of armed miners. The most prominent early expedition was led by Joseph C. Morehead, former quartermaster-general of California, who left San Francisco in April 1851 with 45 men. Supposedly invited to Mexico by citizens in Sonora and Baja California who wanted to be either independent or annexed to the United States, Morehead reached Mazatlán about the end of May. Another group 200 strong arrived in La Paz in June. Morehead's specific goals, however, were imprecise and his followers quickly scattered. Meanwhile his activities had alerted Mexicans, Americans, and the French that portions of Mexico might still be available to those with sounder plans and more perseverance.[4]

In addition to a variety of ambitious adventurers just north of its border, the 1850s were grim years for Sonora. The Apaches were restless and their sporadic raids occurred at a particularly inopportune time, as Mexicans staggered from their defeat in the recent war with the United States. Many citizens of Sonora, ironically ignoring their own land's wealth, were lured north by Californian gold, and this exodus drained the militia needed to oppose the Apaches.

3. For a dramatic recitation of Sonora's problems during the early 1850s, see Governor Aguilar's "Proclamation to Sonora," Ures, July 11, 1856, Mexico City, *Integridad Nacional,* July 18, 1856, reprinted in *Pinart Transcripts, Sonora,* V, 313-15, 318-19.

4. Bancroft, *History of California,* VI, 584; J. Fred Rippy, *The United States and Mexico* (New York: F. S. Crofts, 1931), pp. 87-88; "Monthly Record of Current Events," *Harper's New Monthly Magazine* 19 (December 1851): 124; Joseph Allen Stout, Jr., *The Liberators: Filibustering Expeditions into Mexico, 1848-1862* (Los Angeles: Westernlore Press, 1973), p. 46; and Rufus Kay Wyllys, *The French in Sonora, 1850-1854: The Story of French Adventurers from California into Mexico* (Berkeley: University of California Press, 1932), pp. 52-56

Quarrelsome political factions created destructive civil strife, and Sonora's distressed appeals for military aid from a national government preoccupied with other problems were largely ignored.[5]

Although officials in both Sonora and Mexico City viewed colonists favorably, provided they were not from the United States, they were financially unable to support Mexican military colonies which could have ameliorated their problems. A feasible alternative, to use European colonists to stabilize Sonora's frontiers, would potentially ward off the two greatest threats: Apaches and Anglo-Americans. However, Europeans were attracted by Sonora's mineral wealth, rather than such an altruistic aim as safeguarding Mexico. This irreconcilability of basic objectives later caused countless disputes. Nevertheless, Mexico made appeals to the nearest source of European immigrants, disillusioned gold-seekers in California.[6] Those who responded were primarily French. Within the six month period from November 1851 to May 1852, while France was moving from a republic to an empire, three separate French expeditions left San Francisco for Sonora.

Stimulated by the abortive Morehead attempt in 1851, the Mexican vice-consul at San Francisco, William Schleiden, enlisted Charles de Pindray, a thirty-five-year-old French count, to establish a European frontier colony in Sonora.[7] Pindray had arrived in Massachusetts in 1846 and three years later had journeyed to

---

5. Bancroft, *History of Mexico,* V, 576-80; John Russell Bartlett, *Personal Narrative of Explorations and Incidents in Texas, New Mexico, California, Sonora, and Chihuahua,* 2 vols. (New York: D. Appleton, 1854), II, 302, 385; Bancroft, *North Mexican States,* II, 655-64, 670-72; and Bancroft, *History of California, 1848-1859,* VI, 113.

6. Mariano Paredes, *Proyectos de leyes sobre colonización y comercio en el estado de Sonora, presentados a la Cámara de Diputados, por el representante de aquel estado, en la sesión extraordinario del día 16 de Agosto de 1850* (México: Imprenta de I. Cumplido, 1850). For a translation of Paredes, see Odie B. Faulk, ed., "A Colonization Plan for Northern Sonora, 1850," *New Mexico Historical Review* 44 (October 1969): 293-314; Bancroft, *North Mexican States,* II, 744; and Bancroft, *History of California, 1848-1859,* VI, 407.

7. Pindray's title is given both as count and marquis; Mexican documents generally refer to him as count. Lambertie, *Le drame de Sonora,* pp. 207-09; Lachapelle, *Le comte de Raousset-Boulbon,* pp. 52-55; and Madelène, *Le comte Gaston de Raousset-Boulbon,* p. 53.

California, where he unsuccessfully tried to obtain gold.[8] Patrice Dillon, the French consul in San Francisco, encouraged his countryman to lead an expedition; and, with promises of a favorable reception, Pindray and eighty-eight Frenchmen left California for Sonora on November 21, 1851, aboard the *Cumberland.* During the same month that Louis Napoleon effected his coup d'état, in December 1851, they landed at Guaymas. Mexican officials granted them, and over sixty reinforcements who later joined the group, three leagues of land near the deserted mission at Cocóspera in northern Sonora. After a tedious trip, they reached their destination in March 1852. Harassed by Apaches, the French were further annoyed by a lack of additional Mexican support. As disillusioned members of the expedition began to abandon Pindray and Mexico, the French leader despairingly went to Ures, more than half the way back to Guaymas, in a futile effort to get Mexican aid for his floundering colony.[9] On his return trip to Cocóspera, while spending the night at Rayón on June 5, 1852, Pindray was mysteriously shot—whether by himself, his disgruntled compatriots, or by disaffected Mexicans, is not known.[10]

French diplomats in Mexico had clearly vacillated in their support of Pindray. André Levasseur, the French minister to Mexico, initially encouraged this first French expedition. In January 1852, he and General Miguel Blanco, commandant general of Sonora, even talked of employing Pindray to explore the mineral resources of their mutual

---

8. Horacio Sobarzo, *Crónica de la aventura de Raousset Boulbon en Sonora* (México: Librería de Manuel Porrúa, S.A., 1954), pp. 43-52; and Maurice Soulié, *The Wolf Cub: The Great Adventure of Count Gaston de Raousset-Boulbon in California and Sonora, 1850-1854,* (Indianapolis: Bobbs-Merrill, 1927), pp. 80-89.

9. Wyllys, *The French in Sonora,* p. 71; Lambertie, *Le drame de la Sonora,* pp. 207-10; Appeal to Sonoran government for help from Charles de Pindray, chief of the French colony of Cocóspera, April 4, 1852, Ures, *El Sonorense,* May 14, 1852, *Pinart Transcripts, Sonora,* V, 11; Blanco to the state and to the governor of Sonora, Arispe, May, 1852, *El Sonorense,* June 11, 1852, ibid., p. 28; and Sobarzo, *Crónica de la aventura,* pp. 52-53.

10. Alfred Lachapelle believes by one of his own men, Ernest Vigneaux thinks by Mexican officials, Saint Amant concludes the death is a suicide, and Madelène simply states, "Un mystère." See Bancroft, *North Mexican States,* II, 676, and Lachapelle, *Raousset-Boulbon,* pp. 64-65, for various theories.

interest, the *Compañía Restauradora de la Mina de la Arizona*.[11] The following month the French minister indicated to José Calvo, the French vice-consul at Guaymas, that Pindray could help explore and take possession of the Arizona mine. In this February letter Levasseur informed Calvo of dispatches he had received from Paris instructing him to attract Frenchmen in California to Sonora.[12] However, this enthusiasm and support quickly waned after the arrival in Mexico City in March 1852 of a rival to Pindray, Count Gaston Raoul de Raousset-Boulbon.[13] In April Levasseur wrote Calvo that Pindray's reputation was questionable and that the expedition was "only a feeble advance guard . . . of a considerable body of French emigrants." Switching his support from Pindray to Raousset-Boulbon, he urged the French vice-consul to do likewise.[14] Blanco, Levasseur's mining partner in Sonora, then withheld additional Mexican support from the struggling Pindray group. Finally, Oliver de Lachapelle, Pindray's lieutenant and subsequent leader of the dwindling expedition, joined with Pindray's antagonist, Raousset-Boulbon, in September 1852.[15]

A second French expedition to Sonora was arranged by Lepine de Sigondis, agent of a company promoted in Paris by Pierre Charles de Saint-Amant, the French consular agent at Sacramento. Little is known of this French mining colony whose sixty to eighty men left San Francisco in March 1852, the same month that Pindray reached Cocóspera and Raousset-Boulbon arrived in Mexico City. T. P. Sainte-Marie, later French vice-consul at Acapulco, commanded this

---

11. Blanco to Raousset-Boulbon, September 24, 1852, *El Sonorense*, October 22, 1852, *Pinart Transcripts, Sonora*, V, 98.

12. Levasseur to Calvo, February 28, 1852, Wyllys, *French in Sonora*, appendix B, pp. 249-50.

13. The name of the family is said to have been changed in 1793 from Bourbon to Boulbon, giving rise to the legend that Count Gaston was the natural son of a Bourbon prince. Ibid., pp. 68, 71.

14. Levasseur to Calvo, April 19, 1852, ibid., pp. 250-53.

15. Blanco to Raousset-Boulbon, Arispe, September 24, 1852, *El Sonorense*, October 22, 1852, *Pinart Transcripts, Sonora*, V, 98. Blanco reminded Raousset that he was responsible for the unfavorable reports concerning Pindray. Luis Redondo, prefect of Guadalupe, to Cubillas, September 10, 1852, Ures, *El Sonorense*, October 1, 1852, ibid., p. 71; and Lachapelle, *Le comte de Raousset-Boulbon*, p. 66. The author, Alfred Lachapelle, was the brother of the leader, Oliver, who joined Raousset-Boulbon in September 1852.

group. The colonists landed at Guaymas on April 5; but, like the Pindray force, their numbers soon dwindled as they either returned to California or joined the next French expedition.[16]

Raousset-Boulbon organized the third French group in 1852. He was particularly persistent and came very close to conquering Sonora. He had arrived in San Francisco on August 22, 1850. Finding no fulfillment there, and encouraged by the French consul, he left for Mexico about eighteen months later. Raousset-Boulbon differed significantly from Charles de Pindray and Lepine de Sigondis. Instead of striking out directly for Sonora, he first secured political, financial, and diplomatic backing. Leaving San Francisco for Mexico City on February 17, 1852, he obtained permission and grants in Sonora from the central government. These included a concession from President Mariano Arista for the silver mines of Arizona, the famous *Planchas de Plata* (or *Bolas de Plata*) located on the northern border of Sonora.[17]

Returning to California, Raousset-Boulbon methodically collected about two hundred of his countrymen. Warmly welcomed at Guaymas on June 1, 1852, four days before the mysterious death of Pindray, he confidently began his march northward to the mines. However, conflict soon became evident between the central government at Mexico City and the Sonoran government. Resident officials were reluctant to permit more Frenchmen into their state until the question was resolved as to whether the central or local government had the power to make land and mine concessions.[18]

Another complicating factor for the French was Britain's Barron, Forbes and Company, the financial rival of Raousset-Boulbon's sponsor, the banking house of Jecker de la Torre. Disturbed by this French economic invasion, Eustaquio Barron, British consul at Mazatlán, and William Forbes, British consul at Tepic, began pressuring the

---

16. Wyllys, *French in Sonora*, pp. 64-67.
17. These silver deposits, discovered about 1736 and claimed by local officials for the king of Spain, were closed to individual miners five years later by royal decree. Bancroft, *North Mexican States*, II, 525-28; Lachapelle, *Le comte de Raousset-Boulbon*, p. 87; and Lambertie, *Le drame de Sonora*, pp. 14-17.
18. *El Sonorense*, June 25, and September 24, 1852, *Pinart Transcripts, Sonora*, V, 31-33, 67-69; Fernando Cubillas, governor of Sonora, to the state congress of Sonora, Ures, September 23, 1852, *El Sonorense*, October 1, 1852, ibid., pp. 72-76; and *Annuaire des Deux Mondes*, 1852, pp. 716-17.

Sonoran officials who supported the Jecker enterprise. While Raousset-Boulbon had little control over these political and financial complexities, he indiscreetly flaunted the military appearance of his expedition. A veteran of the Algerian wars, the count marched north to the mines with sword at the ready, leading his column arrayed in full military formation, with fixed bayonets and artillery. A bit more display than appeared necessary to confront Apaches, this third French group particularly disquieted Sonoran officials.[19]

Complicated disputes with Mexican officials ensued. The French minister to Mexico earnestly appealed to both Blanco and Calvo, and then persuaded President Arista to intervene in Raousset-Boulbon's behalf. The French count, however, became exasperated with the delays.[20] In October 1852, the same month that the prince-president of France assuringly stated, "The Empire means peace," Raousset-Boulbon ordered "Liberty to Sonora" inscribed on a tricolor banner, and proceeded to engage the Mexicans in battle, shouting "En avant! Vivé la France!"[21] The startled Sonorans succumbed, and the French force of two hundred men successfully occupied Hermosillo, the largest town in Sonora with a population of about twelve thousand. However, Raousset-Boulbon became seriously ill and, within five months after arriving in Sonora, the French force capitulated.[22]

---

19. Wyllys, *French in Sonora*, p. 77, 92.
20. Madelène, *Le comte Gaston de Raousset-Boulbon*, pp. 99-100; and Lambertie, *Le drame de Sonora*, pp. 76-77. For a sympathetic view, see Gonzalez, Prefect, to Count Raousset-Boulbon, San Ignacio, September 30, 1852, *El Sonorense*, October 8, 1852, *Pinart Transcripts, Sonora*, V, 78-80. For demands, see Acting Governor Cubillas to Raousset-Boulbon, Ures, October 2, 1852, *El Sonorense*, October 15, 1852, ibid., pp. 84-93.
21. Madelène, *Le comte Gaston de Raousset-Boulbon*, pp. 93, 96, 99-100; and Lambertie, *Le drame de Sonora*, pp. 72-74, 76-77.
22. Manuel María Gándara, Centralist governor of Sonora, to Minister of War, Ures, October 26, 1853, *El Nacional*, March 17, *Pinart Transcripts, Sonora*, V, 206; Ures, *La Voz del Pueblo*, November 24, 1852, ibid., pp. 103-04; Blanco to governor of Sonora, Guaymas, November 5, 1852, *El Sonorense*, November 12, 1852, ibid., V, 114; Raousset-Boulbon to Blanco, October 29, 1852, asking for interview with Calvo and Blanco, *El Sonorense*, November 12, 1852, ibid., pp. 110-11; Blanco to Raousset-Boulbon, October 30, 1852, includes terms for French capitulation, ibid., pp. 111-12; "Capitulation of Count Gaston de Raousset-Boulbon", Guaymas, November 4, 1852, *El Sonorense*, November 19, 1852, ibid., pp. 116-19.

Returning to San Francisco in November 1852, they were feted as heroes in France.[23]

During Raousset-Boulbon's short time in Sonora, he had not neglected the silver mines. Sixteen days after the second French empire was formally decreed on December 2, 1852, a rich specimen of silver from the Arizona mine was shown to the editor of the French newspaper in California, the *Echo du Pacifique*. Lauding the purity of the silver and the wealth of other neglected mines, the editor exulted, "The French expedition . . . has served to verify the opinion of the immense wealth of Sonora."[24] This report intrigued the government in Paris, as the scarcity of silver in France had become pronounced: in 1852, for the first time since the Restoration, France had exported more silver than had been imported.[25]

Raousset-Boulbon's dramatic actions in Sonora stimulated discussion in the United States Senate. Michigan's Lewis Cass alleged that the expedition had been directed to acquire Sonora for France. Astutely noting Dommartin's support for French colonization of Sonora, now aided by the French minister to Mexico, Cass correlated this with the *Annuaire des Deux Mondes'* commendation of Levasseur's recent efforts.[26]

In 1853 continued help for Raousset-Boulbon from the French minister to Mexico had become significant. Levasseur had twice obtained President Arista's support for his protégé before Raousset-Boulbon's aggressive behavior was clear.[27] After the French occupation of Hermosillo in October 1852, Mexicans in both Sonora and

---

23. Raousset-Boulbon was permitted to remain in Mexico until early Spring of 1853 when he regained his health. Wyllys, *French in Sonora*, p. 132. *La Voz del Pueblo* (November 24, 1852) criticized the lenient treatment given the French, and conservatively estimated that the above events would "fill one or more pages in the world's history," *Pinart Transcripts, Sonora*, V, 119a. For French evaluation, see *Annuaire des Deux Mondes*, 1852, p. 719.

24. Wyllys, *French in Sonora*, p. 141, citing the *Daily Alta California*, December 18, 1852; and Lachapelle, *Le comte de Raousset-Boulbon*, p. 143.

25. *Enquête sur les principes et les faits généraux qui régissent la circulation monétaire et fiduciaire*, VI, 534-35.

26. *Congressional Globe*, 32nd Cong., 2nd sess., vol. 26, appendix, p. 92.

27. Lambertie, *Le drame de Sonora*, pp. 12-17, 76-77; Lachapelle, *Le comte de Raousset-Boulbon*, pp. 87, 91-98; Wyllys, *French in Sonora*, pp. 72, 256-57; and Madelène, *Le comte Gaston de Raousset-Boulbon*, p. 65.

Mexico City were obviously and justifiably upset. The insurgent could easily have been disavowed and dismissed as an impetuous and incorrigible adventurer. Instead, Levasseur again urged Raousset-Boulbon to return to Mexico City, and he introduced him to yet another Mexican president, Antonio López de Santa Anna, who took office in March 1853, two months after Arista's resignation.[28]

Raousset-Boulbon met with Santa Anna in June 1853. Although the Mexican president was cordial and interested, the two men came to an impasse over the division of the mines.[29] Again disgusted with Mexican politicians, Raousset-Boulbon returned to San Francisco in December 1853, the same month that the signing of the Gadsden Treaty allotted even more Mexican territory to the United States. Throughout the first months of 1854, while France was pledging to guarantee Ottoman integrity and independence from Russian domination, Raousset-Boulbon was recruiting Europeans to take Sonora by force.[30]

He ran into unexpected opposition in California. As the French count arrived in San Francisco after his unproductive talks with President Santa Anna, Major General John E. Wool became commander of the Pacific division of the United States Army. Even before leaving the East for his new post, he had asked for clarification concerning

28. Wyllys, *French in Sonora,* p. 148, citing French minister to Sainte-Marie, French vice-consul in Acapulco, Mexico, April 8, 1853; and French minister to Dillon, Mexico, April 6, 1853.

29. Hypolite Coppey, *El Conde Raousset-Boulbon en Sonora,* (México: Librería de Manuel Porrua, S.A., 1962), p. 38; Lachapelle, *Le comte de Raousset-Boulbon,* p. 143; Madelène, *Le comte Gaston de Raousset-Boulbon,* p. 111; Lambertie, *La drame de Sonora,* p. 99; and Raousset-Boulbon to Santa Anna, Mexico, July 21, 1853, cited by Wyllys, *French in Sonora,* p. 150.

30. As Raousset-Boulbon made preparations to leave San Francisco, Mexico City newspapers published his intercepted correspondence, while Manuel María Gándara, governor of Sonora, heatedly referred to him as "the French *cabecilla.*" Ures, *El Nacional,* March 17, 1854, *Pinart Transcripts, Sonora,* V, 226; and Lambertie, *Le drame de Sonora,* p. 88. For more on Raousset-Boulbon, see William A. Rives, U.S. minister to France, to Edward Everett, U.S. secretary of state, Jan 6, 1853, William R. Manning, ed., *Diplomatic Correspondence of the United States: Inter-American Affairs,* 1831-1860, 10 vols. (Washington, Carnegie Endowment for International Peace, 1937), VI, 643, doc. 2631. Also on Raousset-Boulbon, see ibid., V, 524-25, 576-80, docs. 4090, 4122-24.

filibustering activities against Mexico. Unequivocally instructed to deter such expeditions, Wool took his assignment seriously.[31] Arriving in San Francisco on February 14, 1854, his first dispatch concerned filibusters. Within two weeks he reported, "I am in hopes to be able to arrest Raousset, and prevent him from his lawless purpose."[32] Although Wool failed to stop the renewed French expedition that left San Francisco for Guaymas on April 1, his successful harassment of Raousset-Boulbon inconveniently, and perhaps fatally, delayed his personal departure for seven weeks.

On April 20, the first shipload of 480 men, most of whom had served under the French flag, arrived at Guaymas. Having only half that number to defend the port city, Sonora's commandant general, José María Yáñez, was understandably nervous as he helplessly watched the armed men disembark. He also knew that in San Francisco an additional contingent was preparing to embark for Sonora, supposedly for precious metals but actually, Yáñez feared, for Sonora itself. This danger of reinforcements alarmed both Mexican and United States authorities.[33]

Raousset-Boulbon, detained in San Francisco, did not leave until May 23 on a small and misnamed schooner, the *Belle*, carrying eight men, 180 rifles, and an assortment of ammunition. Writing to both Dillon and Levasseur that he was going back to obtain freedom for Sonora, the irrepressible French count arrived in Guaymas around the first of July.[34] Reluctant to display fear in front of the Frenchmen who

31. Wool to Jefferson Davis, secretary of war, December 26, 1853, *Senate Ex. Doc.*, 33rd Cong., 2nd sess., vol. 6, ser. 751, doc. 16, pp. 3-4; Wool to Davis, January 10, 1854; Davis to Wool, January 12, 1854, ibid., p. 7.
32. Wool to Major General Winfield Scott, Commander, U.S. Army, New York, February 14, 1854, ibid., pp. 9-10; Wool to Lieutenant Colonel L. Thomas, Assistant Adjutant General, Headquarters of the Army, New York, February 28, 1854, *House Ex. Doc.*, 35th Cong., 1st sess., vol. 10, ser. 956, doc. 88, p. 9.
33. For a dramatic protrayal of Yáñez's problems, see Ures, *El Nacional*, August 4, 1854, *Pinart Transcripts, Sonora*, V, 230-34; Wool to Thomas, June 14, 1854, *Senate Ex. Doc.*, 33rd Cong., 2nd sess., vol. 6, ser. 751, doc. 16, pp. 74-76; and James Gadsden, U.S. legation, Mexico, to Wool, August 2, 1854, ibid., p. 107.
34. Lachapelle, *Le comte de Raousset-Boulbon*, pp. 171-77; and Wyllys, *French in Sonora*, p. 192, citing the *Daily Alta California*, September 24, 1854.

boldly drilled daily just outside of Guaymas, Yáñez urgently requested that his appeals for help from Mexico City be kept secret. Apprehensive about the numerical superiority of the invaders, as well as a retaliation by Napoleon III if French citizens were attacked, the Mexicans hesitated to provoke an incident. However, fighting did begin on July 13, shortly after Raousset Boulbon's arrival, and the French were surprisingly defeated.[35] A month later, on August 11, 1854, the Mexicans executed Raousset-Boulbon, who had philosophically expressed his belief that he was always either "too early or too late," as a conspirator.[36]

• • •

The difference between a hero and a visionary is often success or failure. In the 1830s Sam Houston had detached Texas from Mexico's northeastern frontier and in the 1840s John C. Frémont had disengaged California from Mexico's northwestern territory. Both men were acclaimed as daring heroes. In the 1850s six expeditions, three of them associated with France, attempted in various degrees to wrest Sonora from Mexico. Raousset-Boulbon, often considered a quixotic failure, probably had more support from the French government than it was willing to admit. Almost certainly, he influenced French decisions in the 1860s.

Raousset-Boulbon's objectives in Mexico have puzzled scholars from Mexico, the United States, and France. He had made two trips to Mexico City and he had led two expeditions to Sonora. Ostensibly, his purpose was to reactivate Sonora's mines. For this privilege he promised to encourage European colonization, benefiting Mexico by repulsing both Apaches and Anglo-Americans. It seemed a rather simple arrangement that would profit both parties. But neither the

---

35. *El Nacional,* July 15, 1854, *Pinart Transcripts, Sonora,* V, 236-40; Mexico City, *Integridad Nacional,* ibid., p. 341; and Yáñez to minister of war, July 30, 1854, "A full official report of the actions fought on the 13th at Guaymas with Raousset-Boulbon and the Frenchmen," Ures, *El Nacional,* August 25, 1854, ibid., pp. 241-46.

36. Niceto de Zamacois, *Historia de Mejíco desde sus tiempos mas remotos hasta nuestros días,* 18 vols. (México and Barcelona, [1880-1882]), XII, 789; Bancroft, *North Mexican States,* II, 690; General Yáñez in circular of August 13, to prefects, Ures, *El Nacional,* August 18, 1854, *Pinart Transcripts, Sonora,* V, 248; *El Nacional,* September 1, 1854, ibid., pp. 249-50; and Lachapelle, *Le comte de Raousset-Boulbon,* p. 3.

French count nor the Mexican authorities trusted each other, and their justified suspicions led to animosity and hostility. While Raousset-Boulbon did not forthrightly claim the French government's official support, there was often the implied hint that he was fulfilling an important assigned mission.

His correspondence, intercepted in January 1854 at Mazatlán, included an intriguing letter to a French sea captain in Sinaloa named Salar. Instructing him to dissuade Mexicans from feeling like dupes of French schemes, Raousset-Boulbon wrote, "The end does not vary, it remains the same; the means change with the circumstances. . . . In a word, by all means possible, at whatever price . . . see to it that I can get on Mexican soil. The rest will take care of itself."[37] The Mexican minister of war, Santiago Blanco, believed that Raousset-Boulbon's second trip to Sonora was an attempt to overthrow the authorities there and then to claim French protection on the basis of innocently defending himself. As skeptical as Blanco of Raousset-Boulbon's objectives, the United States consul in Guaymas, Major Richard Roman, had instructions to protest against the expected annexation of Sonora by France and to threaten United States intervention.[38]

Although allegations were made in the United States Congress that Raousset-Boulbon was an agent of Napoleon, it is precarious to claim a direct connection, a typical difficulty in Second Empire studies.[39] It is on a secondary level, support from both the French consul in San Francisco and the French minister to Mexico, that aid from France is more evident. Dillon furnished Raousset-Boulbon with letters of recommendations to Levasseur, helped recruit Frenchmen for Sonora, and intervened for them in May 1852 when United States customs officials opposed the exporting of weapons.[40] Shortly after

---

37. Raousset-Boulbon to Salar, undated, but context of the letter indicates it was written in the latter part of 1853, Wyllys, *French in Sonora*, appendix C, pp. 275-79.

38. Blanco to Yáñez, Mexico, August 8, 1854; statement of Juan A. Robinson, Roman's predecessor as United States consul at Guaymas, Juan A. Robinson MSS; both cited by ibid., pp. 215, 220.

39. *Congressional Globe*, 32nd Cong., 2nd sess., vol. 36, appendix, p. 92; ibid., 37th Cong., 3rd sess., appendix, pp. 94-100; and Wyllys, *French in Sonora*, p. 226.

40. Madelène, *Le comte Gaston de Raousset-Boulbon*, pp. 64-70; and Lambertie, *Le drame de Sonora*, p. 16.

the capture of Sonora's largest town Raousset-Boulbon informed Dillon, "What has been done may be of great consequence to France and there should be neither negotiations, hesitation, diplomacy nor idle words. What is needed is action—and that must be energetic and swift."[41] Instead of moderating his fellow countryman's enthusiasm, Dillon urged him to prepare more thoroughly for yet another expedition to Sonora.[42]

The French minister to Mexico had also supported the count. When Raousset-Boulbon made his first trip to Mexico City in late February 1852, Levasseur enthusiastically welcomed him. Opening doors to influential persons, the French minister recommended him to President Arista and to the banking house of Jecker de la Torre, the financier of the *Compañía Restauradora de la Mina de la Arizona*.[43] An unsigned letter to Raousset-Boulbon, dated September 8, 1852, mentioned the "many favors" that Levasseur had done for him. Although Sonorans realized that "some high-toned persons" were involved, *El Sonorense* stated, "Sonorans will not allow themselves to be easily subjugated." The commandant general of Sonora emphatically reported on both the support and Levasseur's statement that it would be "a happy event" if Raousset-Boulbon commanded ten thousand men in Sonora instead of a mere two hundred.[44] In Levasseur's correspondence with Calvo, he repeatedly referred to "our national interest" in connection with the expedition. Urging Calvo to help Raousset-Boulbon, Levasseur asserted that the French foreign minister had instructed him to encourage the establishment of Frenchmen in Sonora, as France had a "vital interest" there.[45]

---

41. Raousset-Boulbon to Dillon, undated but context of letter places it between October 14-24, 1852, when he was at Hermosillo, Soulié, *Wolf Cub,* pp. 168-70.

42. Dillon to Calvo, San Francisco, May 4, 1853, Soulié, *Wolf Cub,* p. 177; Madelène, *Le comte Gaston de Raousset-Boulbon,* p. 105; and Lambertie, *Le drame de Sonora,* pp. 85, 87.

43. Lachapelle, *Le comte de Raousset-Boulbon,* p. 87; and Lambertie, *Le drame de Sonora,* pp. 14-17.

44. Ures, *El Sonorense,* September 17, 24, 1852, *Pinart Transcripts, Sonora,* V, 64; and Blanco to Raousset-Boulbon, Arispe, September 24, 1852, *El Sonorense,* October 22, 1852, ibid., p. 97.

45. Levasseur to Calvo, April 19, May 10, and July 21, 1852, Wyllys, *French in Sonora,* appendix B, pp. 250-57.

The crucial test of French support was after the "Liberty to Sonora" and "Vivé la France" episode of October 1852. With the occupation of Hermosillo, the Mexican government was noticeably perturbed about French connections with the elusive count.[46] After the establishment of the empire in December 1852, ministers and government officials under Napoleon III did little, especially in matters pertaining to foreign policy, without either the emperor's direction or approval.

During the spring of 1853 French officials in the Western Hemisphere diligently denied any connection with or protection of Raousset-Boulbon. However, Levasseur sent word through Dillon that Raousset-Boulbon would be summoned back to Mexico "at the proper moment," and he covertly urged patience as plans for Sonora might be damaged by a premature arrival.[47] Levasseur assured Lucas Alamán, Mexican minister of foreign relations, that the French had no designs upon Sonora and that he had even requested a man-of-war from the French Pacific squadron to guard Mazatlán and Guaymas against any French expeditions from California. At this same time Luis Maneyro, the Mexican consul at Havre, believed that Raousset-Boulbon had the approval of French officials and that reinforcements were preparing to leave France, as success in Sonora was openly anticipated in Paris. Lucas Alamán might well have wondered about the actual purpose of the French man-of-war ordered by Levasseur. Despite the French minister's vehement denials of supporting Raousset-Boulbon in May 1853, only a month earlier he had proposed that the French count come to Mexico City for an interview with the new Mexican president, Santa Anna.[48] Although the influence of Mexican officials wavered during this turbulent period, the French minister showed perseverance in recommending Raousset-Boulbon to two Mexican presidents within a one-year period, especially after the notoriety of his seizure of Hermosillo.

The fate of Sonora seemed to rest uncertainly in the hands of Santa

---

46. Alamán to minister of war, May 2, 9, 1853, ibid., pp. 144-45.
47. Levasseur to Dillon, Mexico, April 6, 1853, ibid., appendix B, pp. 144-45.
48. Levasseur to Alamán, Mexico, May 20, 1853; Luis Maneyro, Mexican consul at Havre, to ministro de relaciones, Havre, May 31, 1853, cited in ibid., appendix B, p. 146; Coppey, *El Conde*, p. 38; Lachapelle, *Le comte de Raousset-Boulbon*, p. 143; and Lambertie, *Le drame de Sonora*, p. 99.

Anna. During late 1853, James Gadsden, United States minister to Mexico, negotiated the purchase of Mexican land adjacent to northern Sonora. Concurrently, an ill-fated filibustering expedition by Tennessee's William Walker skirted diplomatic channels and in January 1854 simply proclaimed into existence his Republic of Sonora. Hindering Raousset-Boulbon's recruiting efforts, rumors in San Francisco during early 1854 indicated that the United States had already absorbed Sonora. The French were thus heartened in the spring of 1854 by the Revolution of Ayutla which, expressing dissatisfaction with the disposal of more national territory, opposed and later deposed President Santa Anna.[49]

Officials in Sonora alarmingly protested that Raousset-Boulbon planned to take possession of Sonora "with an armed band."[50] Despite this, the Mexican consul at San Francisco, Luis Del Valle, had received instructions from Santa Anna to recruit Europeans, primarily Frenchmen detached from the count. These were to be enlisted in the Mexican army in Sonora, after renouncing their French citizenship, and given land as colonists to provide security, obviously necessary after the Walker episode.[51] Del Valle duly chartered the British ship *Challenge* to transport them to Guaymas.[52] The vigilant

49. William O. Scroggs, *Filibusters and Financiers: The Story of William Walker and His Associates* (New York: MacMillan, 1916), p. 42; Captain Juan B. Navarro, prefect, to governor commandante general, Guaymas, November 1, 1853, Ures, *El Nacional,* November 4, December 30, 1853, and January 27, 1854, *Pinart Transcripts, Sonora,* V, 207, 215; on March 4, 1854, some sixty men of various nationalities went to Guaymas without passports as they supposed Sonora to be United States territory. Wyllys, *French in Sonora,* p. 167; and Bancroft, *History of Mexico, 1824-1861,* V, 646-59.

50. Manuel Diez de Bonilla, Mexican minister of foreign relations, to Alphonse Dano, French chargé d'affaires at Mexico City, January 17, 1854, *Senate Ex. Doc.,* 33rd Cong., 2nd sess., vol. 6, ser. 751, doc. 16, pp. 43-44.

51. Wool to Thomas, March 31, 1854; Del Valle to Wool, undated; and John S. Cripps, U.S. legation in Mexico, to Wool, April 22, 1854, ibid., pp. 28, 42, 93-94. Estimates on the number to be recruited vary from one to three thousand. The promises to the Frenchmen made by Del Valle are in *El Nacional,* August 4, 1854, *Pinart Transcripts, Sonora,* V, 230-34.

52. Contract between Del Valle and Edward Cavailler and Hector Chauviteau, March 4, 1854, *Senate Ex. Doc.,* 33rd Cong., 2nd sess., vol. 6, doc. 16, p. 33. Cavailler and Chauviteau turned out to be close friends and associates of Raousset. See Wyllys, *French in Sonora,* pp. 174, 216, 271-79, 284-86, for correspondence between Raousset-Boulbon, Chauviteau, and Cavailler.

and zealous Wool believed that Del Valle was "the dupe of the French consul" and that Raousset-Boulbon planned to seize Sonora "either as a revolutionist or in the name of the French government."[53] Arresting the Mexican consul on March 31, 1854, Wool charged him with violation of an 1818 law forbidding enlistment in United States territory for military service of a foreign government.[54]

The dichotomy of Mexican expectations and French objectives are most explicitly seen in the spring of 1854. Frenchmen were not easily detached from Raousset-Boulbon, they balked at renouncing their citizenship, and they had no intentions of merely farming and fighting Apaches. At the very least, they were after all the mineral wealth they could get; at the most they were after Sonora itself. The contractors for the *Challenge,* the ship chartered by the Mexican consul Del Valle, were not disinterested bipartisans. They were close friends and supporters of Raousset-Boulbon. Wool had substantial reason to conjecture that Del Valle was either the collaborator with, or the dupe of, the French consul at San Francisco.

It is at this point, in April 1854, that Raousset-Boulbon, insisting that his establishment of the French in Sonora would be the first step of France toward the occupation of "all this magnificent country," obviously hoped to attract the aid of France. About this same time Del Valle belatedly became alarmed and began warning authorities in Sonora that the count, supported by "many notables of this region," planned to attack Guaymas.[55] Four days later, he asked officials in

---

53. Wool to Cripps, chargé d'affaires, U.S. legation, Mexico, July 29, 1854, *Senate Ex. Doc.,* 33rd Cong., 2nd sess., vol. 6, ser. 751, doc 16, pp. 94-96.

54. Wool to Thomas, March 31, 1854; San Francisco *Herald Extra,* March 31, 1854, ibid., pp. 27-32. The Mexican consul was convicted, but Wool was reprimanded for Del Valle's arrest. See Wool to Davis, April 14, 1854; Davis to Wool, April 14, 1854, ibid., pp. 52-54. However, before Wool received the reprimand, he also arrested the French consul. Dillon was found not guilty as the jury stood ten for conviction and two for acquittal. Wool to Davis, May 30, 1854, ibid., pp. 66-69.

55. Pierre de la Gorce, *Histoire du second empire,* 7 vols. (Paris: Plon-Nourrit et cie, 1874), IV, 15; Madelène (*Le comte Gaston de Raousset-Boulbon,* pp. 105, 111) claims that Raousset-Boulbon maintained an agent in Paris to promote his project at the court of Napoleon III; Del Valle to governor comandante general of Sonora, San Francisco, April 20, 1854, in *El Nacional,* May 26, 1854, *Pinart Transcripts, Sonora,* V, 228.

San Francisco for help, as "good sources" had revealed that Raousset-Boulbon "resolved to carry out his criminal intent of invading the Mexican Coast." Del Valle had reason for his gloomy forebodings. Using rhetoric that Napoleon repeated, Raousset-Boulbon proclaimed that the United States must be curtailed by "planting a new race in Sonora, if not by seizing all of Mexico." If this were not done, he asserted, in ten years there would not be a cannon shot in Europe without the permission of the United States.[56]

Official French help to Raousset-Boulbon in the latter half of 1853 and the first half of 1854 is difficult to pin down because of the complicated deceptiveness of French diplomats. In Mexico City, Alphonse Dano replaced Levasseur as French chargé d'affaires in the summer of 1853. While continuing to support French mining projects in Sonora, Dano appeared steadfast in his disassociation with the French count. His dislike of Raousset-Boulbon did not hinder his own efforts, however, to settle Frenchmen in Sonora. In the summer of 1854, Dano proposed that the four hundred Frenchmen accompanying the invading expedition be permitted to remain in Sonora. To defray their expenses he sent them twenty thousand pesos which had been appropriated by Mexican officials.[57]

Dillon denied association with Raousset-Boulbon only when it was expedient.[58] On March 18, 1854, he remonstrated that he had "the most positive orders," both from Paris and from the legation in Washington, that French filibustering expeditions "would be viewed by

---

56. Del Valle to governor comandante general of Sonora, San Francisco, April 24, 1854, enclosing letter from Del Valle to collector of customs at San Francisco, April 24, 1854, in *El Nacional,* May 26, 1854, ibid., p. 228. This is almost identical to the statements of Lamartine, Napoleon III, and the Marquis de Radepont, ten years later during the French intervention in Mexico. This statement of Raousset-Boulbon is in Soulié, *Wolf Cub,* pp. 190-93.

57. Wyllys, *French in Sonora,* p. 217, citing Yáñez to minister of war, Guaymas, September 4, 1854. Dano reappeared as French minister to Mexico in 1865, again to soothe Mexican nationalism, after his predecessor, the Marquis de Montholon, failed to obtain Sonora's mines for France.

58. Senator J. A. McDougall of California asserted that Dillon's denials of complicity were "carefully worded, which, while it would save the appearance of complicity on the part of the French Emperor, would not seriously injure the prospects of the enterprise." *Congressional Globe,* 37th Cong., 3rd sess., appendix, p. 97.

them with the utmost displeasure as an act of open and barefaced pira-
cy." He appeared indignant that Wool associated him with Raousset-
Boulbon, claiming that he was "merely desirous of his welfare" as both
he and the count had "a common friend" in Paris.[59] Yet less than two
weeks after these strongly worded denials, he urged the vice-consul at
Guaymas to intercede for the Frenchmen who would soon arrive.
Instructing Calvo to assure Sonoran authorities of their "innocent
motives," Dillon ambiguously added that French warships would soon
be along the Pacific coast. Aware of this letter, Wool realized that in spite
of Dillon's previous denials, the French consul did indeed take "a deep
interest" in the success of the expedition.[60] Although Wool's impetuous
arrests of both the Mexican and French consuls in San Francisco caused
confusion in the State Department, it was commonly believed that
Dillon concealed the hidden motives of Raousset-Boulbon.[61]

While French diplomats unquestionably had an extraordinary
interest in the mineral wealth of Sonora, Raousset-Boulbon was even
more candidly encouraged by minor officials. Dr. Pigne Dupuytren,
a former French consular agent at Marysville, was one of the close
friends accompanying Raousset-Boulbon on his last and fatal trip to
Sonora in May 1854. T. P. Sainte-Marie who had commanded the
Sigondis expedition to Sonora in March 1852, settled his men as
colonis vecinos somewhere between Santa Cruz and Tucson, and then
joined Raousset-Boulbon's first thrust into Sonora. After this 1852
failure, Sainte-Marie was appointed French vice-consul at Acapulco
implying, if not French approval, at least no disapproval of his connection with Raousset-Boulbon. In July 1854, while Raousset-
Boulbon was in Guaymas, Sainte-Marie went to Mexico City to dis-
cuss the future of Sonora with the French minister. Nothing came of
these talks and his Santa Cruz colony largely disintegrated.[62]

Nine years after Raousset-Boulbon's execution, as the French were

59. Dillon to Wool, March 18, 20, 1854, *Senate Ex. Doc.*, 33rd Cong., 2nd
    sess., vol. 6, ser. 751, doc. 16, pp. 34, 43.
60. Dillon to Calvo, San Francisco, March 27, 1854, cited by Wyllys, *French in
    Sonora*, p. 185; and Wool to Cripps, July 29, 1854, *Senate Ex. Doc.*, 33rd
    Cong., 2nd sess., vol. 6, ser. 751, doc. 16, pp. 94-96.
61. Wyllys, *French in Sonora*, p. 180.
62. Ibid., pp. 64-65, 192, 199.

thwarted in their efforts to capture Puebla and before there were any military moves toward northern Mexico, California's Senator James A. McDougall warned of the dangers to Sonora. Recalling that French complicity with Raousset-Boulbon had been denied, he asserted that nevertheless the intervention in Mexico in the 1860s stemmed from the count's activities in Sonora during the 1850s.[63] Although the French government's connection with Raousset-Boulbon is largely based on circumstantial evidence, neither he nor his followers were forgotten. Napoleon received many petitions requesting compensation for services rendered to Raousset-Boulbon; "Accordé" was jotted on the margins of nearly all of them. Raousset-Boulbon emerged a hero through sympathetic writings in France which frequently referred to him as the French Cortés, and his remains, exhumed by French naval officers in 1866, were taken to France for final burial.[64]

Occupied with the opening phase of the Crimean War, Napoleon III's direct participation in the Raousset-Boulbon expedition was probably minimal. However, he undoubtedly would have taken advantage of any success, as France's need for silver was already well apparent. During the three years of Raousset-Boulbon's activities in Sonora, France had lost a total of 184 million silver francs in excess of imports. In 1854, the year of Raousset-Boulbon's most serious invasion of Sonora, the intense lack of silver resulted in the least amount of silver coinage in France since 1795.[65]

The primary legacy of Raousset-Boulbon was the stimulation of Napoleon's interest in Sonora, as well as the connection with the financier, Jean Baptiste Jecker, who was to provide the pretext for French intervention in Mexico in 1861. When Jecker needed French support in the late 1850s, he emphasized his association with Raousset-Boulbon, instead of harboring ill will toward the unfortunate expedition he had financially supported. Furthermore, it was not easily forgotten in France that it had taken only two hundred Frenchmen to occupy a Sonoran town with a population of twelve thousand.

---

63. *Congressional Globe*, 37th Cong., 3rd sess., appendix, p. 97.

64. Delord, *Histoire du second empire*, III, 288-89; and Wyllys, *French in Sonora*, p. 224, citing an interview with José A. Márquez, Guaymas, November 30, 1928.

65. *Enquête sur la circulation monétaire*, VI, 534-35; and *Hansard's: Currency*, appendix, pp. 86-91.

Chapter Five

Jean Baptiste Jecker
A Catalyst for Intervention

During the years from Raousset-Boulbon's death in Sonora to the French intervention in Mexico, 1854 to 1861, more than two and one half billion francs of silver flowed from France, considerably more than the French had lost in the entire first half of the nineteenth century.[1] Critical monetary problems resulted from this dearth of silver. The situation became even more acute in 1861. With the major source of cotton cut off by the American Civil War, India became the primary producer for the French textile industry. Adding to this discomfiture, Indian suppliers inopportunely demanded payment in silver.

Caught by this monetary and manufacturing dilemma, Napoleon III became intensely interested in Sonora, believed to be one of the richest silver states in Mexico. Raousset-Boulbon had stimulated curiosity and knowledge of Sonora's mines. His financier, Jean Baptiste Jecker, was the catalyst that helped to transform France's lack of silver into a major invasion of Mexico.

Historically, attention has focused on Jecker's bonds. These were of negligible value, however, in comparison to his claims to large portions of Sonora. By assuming protection of Jecker's contracts in Mexico, Napoleon III obtained access to desperately needed silver mines. Faced with losing all of his assets as a result of Mexico's domestic turmoil, the Swiss financier agreed to sell his claims in Sonora to France, in exchange for support of his other investments. In addition,

---

1. From 1815 through 1853, 1,695,000,000 silver francs were exported. Yet during the eight years from 1854 through 1861, 2,514,000,000 silver francs were exported. See appendix on silver imports and exports, taken from "Mouvement des métaux précieux," Enclosure 1 in Decazes to Lyons, April 10, 1876, *Hansard's: Currency,* appendix, pp. 86-87.

other participants in Jecker's surveying enterprise transferred their mining claims to France, also for protection of their other financial ventures in Mexico. Thus, by 1862 Napoleon had systematically laid claim to a sizeable portion of the land surveyed by Jecker, and the silver of Sonora that would alleviate France's problems appeared within reach.

• • •

After Raousset-Boulbon's death in 1854, a spate of books appeared, romanticizing his adventures. Frenchmen quickly purchased the first edition of Henri de la Madelène's *Le comte de Raoussset-Boulbon* in 1856. Significantly, a large part of the 1859 second edition was acquired by J. B. Jecker, Raousset-Boulbon's Swiss financier.[2] In January 1861, the Duc de Morny, president of the *corps législatif,* sent an agent to Mexico for information about his own personal investments in Jecker bonds and mines. In Paris Jecker freely distributed copies of Madelène's book which had glorified Raousset-Boulbon as a valiant French patriot wronged by the Mexican government, thus publicizing his earlier financial association with the deceased count.[3] He then formally exchanged his claims in Sonora for a two million dollar settlement from France.[4]

Jecker had important personal reasons for encouraging French involvement. His Mexican investments and projected financial ventures

---

2. Bancroft, *North Mexican States,* II, 692.
3. Jecker to Eugène Conti, chef du cabinet de l'Empereur, December 8, 1869, A. Poulet-Malassis, ed., *Papiers secrets et correspondance du Second Empire. Réimpression complète de l'édition de l'Imprimerie Nationale, annotée et augmentée de nombreuses pièces publiées à l'étranger, et recueillies par A. Poulet-Malassis,* 3rd ed. (Paris: Ghio et cie, 1873), pp. 1-3, and Bancroft, *North Mexican States,* II, 692. Throughout the 1850s, two other books, in addition to Madelène's, were published about Raousset-Boulbon: Lachapelle, *Le comte de Raousset-Boulbon;* and Lambertie, *Le drame de Sonora.* Also published in the 1850s, noteworthy for their later influence, are Gabriel Ferry, *Impressions de voyages et aventures dans le Mexique, la haute Californie et les régions de l'or* (Paris, 1851); and Mathieu de Fossey, *Le Mexique* (Paris, 1857). A second edition of Fossey's work, often quoted in Jecker's correspondence, was published in Paris in 1862.
4. Jecker sold the French government his claims in Sonora for about 10,600,000 francs. Paul Gaulot, *La vérité sur l'expédition du Mexique, d'après les documents inédits de Ernest Louet, payeur en chef du corps expéditionnaire,* 3 vols. (Paris: P. Ollendorff, 1890), I, 219-20.

were complex and comprehensive. A number of his letters, intercepted and turned over to the United States government, referred to plans involving railroads, canal building, provisioning of the French army, and collection of custom duties. In addition to his mineral claims in Sonora, Jecker also owned other mines, land, and concessions elsewhere in Mexico.[5]

In 1852 Jean Baptiste Jecker first became financially involved with both the French and with the fabled mineral wealth of Sonora. Almost a year before Raousset-Boulbon's first trip to Mexico City, the French minister to Mexico had made formal inquiries regarding the Arizona mine in northern Sonora. He received the concession to this mine on January 17, 1852, a month before the French count left San Francisco. When Raousset-Boulbon arrived, Levasseur recommended him to the banking house of Jecker de la Torre and Company which had expressed an interest in financing the French minister's mining concession. Having formed the *Compañía Restauradora de la Mina de la Arizona,* as a subsidiary of Jecker de la Torre and Company, Jecker perceived that Raousset-Boulbon could be useful in exploring and exploiting mines in Sonora.[6]

According to the contract between Jecker and Raousset-Boulbon, the latter would receive one-half of the land, mines, and placers that he located and described, and the other half would go to the *Compañía Restauradora* whose members, in addition to Jecker, included important Frenchmen and Mexicans: Levasseur, the French minister to Mexico; José Calvo, French vice-consul at Guaymas;

---

5. These intercepted letters are reprinted in *House Ex. Doc.,* 37th Cong., 3rd sess., vol. 5, ser. 1161, doc. 23, pp. 12-25. His holdings in Jalisco and Tehuantepec are noted in M. Maldonado-Koerdell, "La Obra de la commission scientifique du Mexique," Arnáiz y Freg and Bataillon, eds., *La intervencion francesa,* p. 164. His claim to the Santa Anna mine is recorded by the *Comision Cientifica de Pachuca, 1864, dirigida por el ingeniero Ramón Almaraz* (México: J. M. Andrade y F. Escalante, 1865), p. 115.

6. Lachapelle, *Le comte de Raousset-Boulbon,* p. 87; Lambertie, *Le drame de Sonora,* pp. 14-17; and *El Sonorense,* September 24, 1852, in *Pinart Transcripts, Sonora,* V, 67-68. Ernest Vigneaux claimed that Raousset-Boulbon actually formed the company, with Jecker's firm as nominal head. He is probably referring to the *Compagnie de Sonore.* Bancroft, *North Mexican States,* II, 676. Jecker had paid for the damages incurred by Raousset-Boulbon during his 1852 expedition to Sonora. *El Sonorense,* December 3, 1852, in *Pinart Transcripts, Sonora,* V, 128.

Mariano Arista, president of Mexico; and José de Aguilar, governor of Sonora. Other Mexicans in strategic positions of authority were also stockholders in the company. Placing $35,000 at the disposal of Raousset-Boulbon in July 1852, the *Compañía Restauradora* assured him of an additional $25,000 for his expedition. Raousset-Boulbon then formed the *Compagnie de Sonore* in anticipation of obtaining his half of the land and mines as determined by his contract with Jecker.[7] This company, projected to last until January 1, 1856, was formally dissolved under Mexican pressure in November 1852.[8]

Two years after Raousset-Boulbon's execution in 1854, Jecker persevered in obtaining even more concessions. He arranged with the Mexican government to survey the public domain of Sonora in August 1856; in return, he was to receive one-third of the land he surveyed. This time Jecker primarily relied on Americans to contribute money and men. Captain J. B. G. Isham, holding one-fourth interest in this Jecker contract, engaged Captains Whiting and Stone, United States Army engineers, to lead the surveying expedition.[9]

Sonora was rife with problems, and on May 17, 1859, Governor Ignacio Pesqueira expelled the Jecker surveyors.[10] The American investors

---

7. *El Sonorense,* September 17, 1852, ibid., V, 60; Villa, *Historia del Estado de Sonora,* p. 217; and Coppey, *El conde,* p. 10. It is important to note that Levasseur withdrew from the enterprise before Raousset-Boulbon landed at Guaymas, but he continued to support the Frenchman, negating the charge that he supported Raousset-Boulbon only for his own financial gain. See Levasseur to Calvo, April 19, 1852, cited by Wyllys, *French in Sonora,* pp. 130, 761, and Wyllys's evaluation of Levasseur, ibid., pp. 227-28. Bancroft, *North Mexican States,* II, 677n.

8. "Ultimos días del gobierno de Mariano Arista. Diario de los acontecimientos que precedieron y diguieron a la caída de Arista," Lilia Díaz, *Versión francesa de México: Informes diplomáticos,* 4 vols. (México: El Colegio de México, 1963-67), I, 18.

9. The Jecker-Comonfort treaty concerning the survey of Sonora was signed on December 19, 1856. Sobarzo, *Crónica de la aventura de Raousset-Boulbon en Sonora,* p. 13; Gaulot, *La vérité sur l'expédition du Mexique,* I, 219; Villa, *Historia del Estado de Sonora,* p. 273; and Hallie Mae McPherson, *William McKendree Gwin: Expansionist* (Ph.D. diss., University of California, Berkeley, 1931), p. 252.

10. Gaulot, *La vérité sur l'expédition du Mexique,* I, 219. For Sonora's economic, social and political situation between 1854 and 1866, see Stuart F. Voss, *On the Periphery of Nineteenth Century Mexico: Sonora and Sinaloa 1810-1877* (Tucson: University of Arizona Press, 1982) pp. 132-60, 168-74.

bitterly protested, and when Captain Stone appealed to his government for support of the expedition, the United States war vessel *St. Mary* briefly intervened in his behalf. Stone and Whiting then petitioned President James Buchanan for protection but, after some vacillation, the president decided not to interfere.[11] Although Jecker's contract with President Comonfort was deemed null and void in 1859, he persistently maintained his claim to one-third of the public land he had surveyed, as reimbursement of expenses.[12]

To protect his financial investments, Jecker quickly became involved in political and financial affairs in Mexico City during this troubled era of Mexican history. The civil war of 1858-61 produced two rival presidents: the conservative Miguel Miramón and the liberal Benito Juárez. In 1859 Miramón dominated the strategic capital, but he was in dire financial straits, as Juárez controlled the revenue-producing port of Vera Cruz.

Miramón found temporary alleviation from his pecuniary plight on October 29, 1859, when the Swiss financial house of Jecker lent his desperate government $1.5 million in return for $15 million in Mexican treasury bonds. Juárez was equally concerned about funds in 1859. The United States minister to Mexico, Robert McLane, offered the liberal president $4 million for considerable privileges in Sonora and other

---

11. Ramón Corral, *Obras históricas: Reseña histórica del Estado de Sonora, 1856-1877* (Hermosillo: Mexico: Biblioteca sonorense de geografía e historia, 1959), pp. 36-37; McLane to Cass, December 21, 1859, United States National Archives, Department of State, Ministers' Despatches, vol. 28, microcopy 97, roll 29 (hereinafter cited as NA, State, MD Mex.); Gwin to Maximilian, September 1863, Evan J. Coleman, "Senator Gwin's Plan for the Colonization of Sonora," *Overland Monthly,* 2nd ser., 17 (May 1891): 499-501; Mata to Ocampo, September 19, 1859, Léon de Montluc, ed., *Armand de Montluc, correspondance de Juárez et de Montluc, ancien consul général du Mexique, accompagnée de nombreuses lettres de personnages politiques, relatives à l'expédition du Mexique,* 3 vols. (Paris: G. Charpentier et cie, 1885), III, 699-702.

12. Bancroft, *North Mexican States,* II, 676, 695. The participants and claims are intricately involved. For United States citizens involved in the Jecker claims, see "Claims Against Mexico Under the Convention of 1868" (201 envelopes and 5 vols.), *Records of Boundary and Claims Commissions and Arbitrations,* National Archives, RG 76. This includes the claim of the Lower California Company that operated under the concession granted to Jecker. The Lower California Company grant is in the Huntington Library, San Marino, California. For list of claimants and nature of claims, see *Senate Ex. Doc.,* 44th Cong., 2nd sess., vol. 3, ser. 1720, doc. 31.

portions of Mexico.[13] This McLane-Ocampo treaty, signed December 14, 1859, was never ratified by the United States Senate. However, European governments were alarmed by its ramifications which, they alleged, would cause Mexico to be an appendage of the United States. Both the Jecker loan and the McLane-Ocampo treaty reflect the uncertain political conditions in Mexico. While world opinion was indignant about the usurious profits of the Jecker-Miramón contract, the McLane-Ocampo treaty amazed United States newspaper editors who scarcely believed that the proposed concessions could be obtained for such a small sum, in comparison with previous offers and payments for Mexican grants and territory.[14] Alienated over cancellation of his contract to survey Sonora, and hopeful that his claims would be recognized by the conservative president, Jecker financially supported Miramón.

The Jecker bondholders included French, Swiss, and Belgian residents in Mexico. These speculators became nervous when Jecker went bankrupt in May 1860. They became frantic when Juárez defeated his rivals and triumphantly entered Mexico City on January 11, 1861.[15] Temporarily arrested and ordered to leave Mexico, Jecker turned to the members of the diplomatic corps for help. Needing intercession for his claims, Jecker was told by the Swiss consul-general that the United States normally assumed diplomatic protection for Swiss citizens in Mexico. Initially competition developed between his

---

13. Vicente Fuentes Díaz, *La intervencion europa en México, 1861-62* (México: 1962), p. 67. Bonds paying 6 percent interest were issued to the amount of 75,000,000 francs. In return, Miramón was given 3,094,640 francs in cash, 4,344,500 francs in various bonds, custom house orders, military supplies, and 33,000 francs in diverse credits and payments. In 1862 the franc stood at $0.1931. Bock, *Tripartite Convention*, p. 613. The October 29, 1859, contract between Jecker and Miramón is reprinted in Ernesto de la Torre Villar et al., eds., *Historica documental de México*, 2 vols. (México: Universidad Nacional Autonoma de México, 1964), II, 312-13; Zamacois, *Historia de Méjico*, XV, 337-42.

14. See especially Bancroft, *History of Mexico*, V, 773-75; and Díaz, *Versión francesa de México*, II, 123-28.

15. A. de la Londe, to Thouvenel, May 21, 1860, reprinted in Díaz, *Versión francesa de México*, II, 163-64; Mathew to Elger, February 1, 1861, and Mathew to Zarco, February 1, 1861, ibid., 208-13. This was the same month that French coinage of five-franc and two-franc silver pieces, the only silver coins used in transactions of any importance, totally ceased. Willis, *Monetary Union*, p. 39.

supporters, especially the ministers from Prussia and Peru, and the United States minister did intervene for him; but Count Dubois de Saligny, the new French minister to Mexico, extended his country's protection to the Swiss banker with unfeigned alacrity.[16]

Fraught with meaning for France's cotton supply, tension escalated in the United States with the secession of South Carolina in December 1860. During that same month, Saligny arrived in Mexico City, a few weeks ahead of Juárez. The French minister was in the capital only a fortnight when he received a petition from 150 anxious French, Swiss, and Belgian residents, seeking protection for their interests in the Jecker bonds. They found a sympathetic response; Saligny vigorously accepted the defense of their investments. At this very time, in addition to uneasiness about future raw cotton sources, France's lack of silver demanded energetic action. The French press agitated for a solution to the serious export of small coin, and strenuous demands were made for the government to find a remedy.[17]

Saligny had indicated an interest in Jecker's financial affairs even before he left France. After his appointment to Mexico, he had told Xavier Elsesser, Jecker's brother-in-law, that the claims would probably be respected. This protection of a Swiss citizen by the new French minister to Mexico aroused speculation (recently substantiated) about the Duc de Morny's connection with Jecker. However, the supposition that the French government would send six thousand troops to Mexico in 1862 to recover Morny's alleged claim to 30 percent of the Jecker bond profits appears untenable. It is of interest, however, that Morny, the emperor's half-brother, encouraged development of Sonora's mines through both the Swiss Jean Baptiste Jecker and the American William McKendree Gwin, a later agent of Napoleon III.[18]

The French minister arrived in Mexico City with letters accrediting

16. Comte Emile de Kératry, *La créance Jecker, les indemnités françaises et les emprunts mexicains* (Paris: Librairie Internationale, 1868), pp. 18-19; and *House Ex. Doc.,* 37th Cong., 3rd sess., vol. 5, ser. 1161, doc. 23, pp. 1-11.

17. Bock, *Tripartite Convention,* pp. 97-100, 613-14; 631-32; and Willis, *Monetary Union,* pp. 33-34.

18. Xavier Elsesser to Montluc, October 1, 1860, Montluc, *Correspondance de Juárez et de Montluc,* I, 47-49; Nancy N. Barker, "The Duke of Morny and the Affair of the Jecker Bonds," *French Historical Studies* 6 (Fall 1970): 555-61; Coleman, "Gwin's Plan," *Overland Monthly* 17 (June 1891): 606; and ibid. 18 (August 1891): 204-06.

him to the defeated Miramón. Saligny failed in his attempt to withhold French recognition of the new government until it acknowledged the Jecker claims as a legitimate Mexican debt. Juárez desired French recognition, but not desperately enough to pay $15 million. Having been in Mexico more than three months without being formally received, Saligny capitulated, presenting his credentials on March 16, 1861. He was as yet unaware that ten days earlier the French foreign minister, Edouard Antoine Thouvenel, had unequivocally directed him to have the Jecker claims acknowledged.[19] The critical issues of cotton and silver perhaps influenced Thouvenel's dispatch since only one month earlier, in February 1861, the Confederate States of America had been formed. A war between the states was imminent, and France defensively prepared to meet its ramifications.

Meanwhile, on the basis of previous instructions, Saligny diligently tried to secure Mexican recognition of the Jecker claims. While negotiations affecting other French claims were impeded because of the impasse involving Jecker, Saligny engaged in a diplomatic duel with Francisco Zarco, Juárez's minister of foreign relations. Zarco was an admirable opponent. When the French minister argued "loudly and firmly," Zarco finally agreed, orally, that he would accept, "in principle," Mexican responsibility for the bonds and that he would arrange "the bases of a nature to satisfy M. Jecker." The ambiguity of this did not escape Saligny who pressed for a written guarantee. To this demand, however, Zarco deftly demurred that certain delays were necessary.[20] When the Mexican government would not ratify Zarco's agreement, Saligny became more belligerent. Having recognized Juárez before he received Thouvenel's explicit instructions of March 6, Saligny had depleted his diplomatic resources. Six weeks after establishing French relations with the new liberal government, Saligny made his first official request for a French force, "sufficient in power no matter what happens, for the protection of our interest."[21] Sixteen days earlier, the American Civil War had begun.

---

19. Thouvenel to Saligny, March 6, 1861, cited by Bock, *Tripartitie Convention,* pp. 100-01, 123.
20. Saligny to Thouvenel, March 28, 1861, Díaz, *Versión francesa de México,* II, 220-23. See Saligny-Zarco Convention, March 26, 1861, reprinted in Bock, *Tripartite Convention,* appendix E, pp. 491-94.
21. Saligny to Thouvenel, April 28, 1861, Díaz, *Versión francesa de México,* II, 231-35.

Shortly after his plea for French force, Saligny met with the minister of foreign relations and with José María Mata, the minister of finance. Mata, as adept as Zarco at making oral promises, assured the French minister that he would defend the Jecker claims in the Mexican congress. Saligny then threatened the two Mexican ministers that if the Jecker claims were not honored, France might sever diplomatic relations, with consequences that "would lead to the ruin of your Government and your country." Six days after his conference with Zarco and Mata, the French minister again requested help from Paris. Asserting that if his government would send gunboats "armed with long-range cannons, . . . I would very well make the dignity and rights of France respected," Saligny proposed that he himself be authorized to employ this force, "according to the necessities of circumstance."[22] Clearly, Jecker supporters had substantial reason to remark that Saligny was "so useful." Concurrent with Saligny's demands, a monetary debate ensued in the French senate in May 1861 about the total lack of silver coin, and the senate urged the ministry of finance to take "immediate action" to rectify the shortage.[23]

Franco-Mexican relations continued to deteriorate. Zarco resorted to his previously successful tactic, delay. The problem, he insisted, was that he lacked authority; recognition of French claims had to be approved by the Mexican congress which had not yet convened. This failed to mollify Saligny who tenaciously demanded written guarantees. Zarco finally appeared to submit when he wrote to the French minister that Mexico would adhere to "the principles of international law." In need of a diplomatic triumph, Saligny prematurely exulted over this "written recognition of the principle that we are defending."[24] His elation was short lived. To his dismay, Mexican foreign ministers resigned with startling rapidity. Zarco, from whom he had finally extracted a written statement, resigned eight days later, on May 9, 1861. His successor, Leon Guzmán, would not accept Zarco's concession, although he assured Saligny that he would also resign if unable to settle the Jecker claims. Guzmán duly

---

22. Saligny to Thouvenel, May 7, 1861, cited by Bock, *Tripartite Convention,* p. 101.
23. Louis Elsesser, nephew of Jecker, to Jecker, August 31, 1862, *House Ex. Doc.,* 37th Cong., 3rd sess., vol. 5, ser. 1161, doc. 23, p. 12; and Horn, "La crise monétaire," pp. 6-7.
24. Saligny to Thouvenel, May 9, 1861, cited by Bock, *Tripartite Convention,* pp. 101-02, 633.

resigned on June 17. For almost a month, until July 13, there was no Mexican foreign minister; the chargé ad interim, Palacio y Magarola, skillfully maintained that he had no authority to decide anything concerning French affairs. Saligny, incensed at these disappearing foreign ministers who so adeptly abjured responsibility, complained that negotiation about French claims was a "bad joke that has lasted too long."[25]

Intermittently threatening Mexico with termination of French diplomatic relations, Saligny increasingly punctuated his dispatches to Paris with appeals for force. On July 17, 1861, the financially harassed Mexican congress passed a law suspending interest payment on all foreign debts for two years. In the stormy period that followed, the French minister claimed that the Mexican law was a "new insult, free and premeditated against France." Abrasively demanding annulment of the law within twenty-four hours, Saligny severed diplomatic relations on July 25, 1861.[26]

Four days later, the United States minister to Mexico, Thomas Corwin, suggested that his country lend money to Mexico for eradication of its foreign debts. The collateral Corwin recommended was all public lands and mineral rights in Sonora, Lower California, Chihuahua, and Sinaloa. He forthrightly wrote the secretary of state, William Henry Seward, "This would probably end in the cession of the sovereignty to us. It would be certain to end thus if the money were not promptly paid as agreed on." The goals of Raousset-Boulbon, Jecker, and Napoleon III thus resembled those of Corwin, who reminded Seward of Sonora's mineral wealth.[27] Seward then told

---

25. Saligny to Thouvenel, May 18, June 22 and June 29, 1861, Díaz, *Versión francesa de México,* II, 238-41, 252-56, 258-60.

26. Saligny to Thouvenel, July 17 and 27, 1861, ibid., pp. 260-67; and William Spence Robertson, "The Tripartite Treaty of London," *Hispanic American Historical Review* 20 (May 1940): 168.

27. Corwin to Seward, July 29 and August 28, 1861, NA, State, MD Mex., vol. 28 (December 21, 1859-February 5, 1862), microcopy 97, roll 29. Earlier, in 1857, Lewis Cass, had instructed the minister to Mexico, John Forsyth, to try to buy Lower California, Sonora and part of Chihuahua. Cass to Forsyth, July 17, 1857 in Manning, IX, doc. 3921, pp. 234-38. See also Auguste T'Kint de Roodenbeke (sic., Roodenbeek) to de Vrière, October 28, 1861, Belgium, Archives du Ministère des Affaires étrangères, Correspondance politique, Mexique, vol. I (hereinafter cited as AEB, CP, Mex.) no. 40. The loan scheme is in Hanna and Hanna, *Napoleon III and Mexico,* pp. 53-55, 71-72.

Lord Edmund Lyons, British minister at Washington, that the United States would pay the two years' interest on all Mexican foreign debts, in exchange for mortgages on certain Mexican territory. When Corwin related this to Juárez, however, the offer was declined.[28] Six months later, with French, Spanish, and British troops actually on Mexican soil, Juárez changed his mind and signed an appropriate treaty with the United States on April 6, 1862. This further agitated the French who heatedly protested on the basis that they already had claims to the land proposed as collateral.[29]

With Sonora coveted by both the United States and France, the Jecker claims and Mexico's suspension of international payments served as pretexts for French intervention. When Lord Cowley, British minister to France, protested exorbitant demands made by Saligny, as well as Napoleon's protection of Jecker, the French emperor admitted that he himself had insisted the claims be made excessive, to prohibit Juárez's acceptance of a settlement.[30] This is corroborated by corollary French actions. More than a month before the Mexican congress refused to honor the Jecker claims, the French foreign minister had investigated potential naval support. The French minister of marine and colonies assured Thouvenel on July 2, 1861, fifteen days before Mexico suspended international interest payments, that his request could be satisfied.[31]

---

28. Corwin received these instructions on September 27, 1861. Bancroft, *History of Mexico,* VI, 22-23n. Also see the P.S. to Blondeel van Cuelebroeck to de Vrière, November 7, 1861, AEB, CP, Mex., no. 230, as well as Seward's December 4, 1861 response to Spanish, French and British ministers, a copy enclosed in Blondeel to Rogier, December 15, 1861, ibid., no. 239. Also note Blondeel to Rogier, December 7, 1861, ibid., no. 235.

29. Romero to Seward, February 6, 1865, reminding Seward of the French protests of April 15, 1862, *House, Ex. Doc.,* 39th Cong., 1st sess., vol. 1, pt. 3, ser. 1246, doc. 1, pp. 500-02.

30. Cowley-Napoleon III Conversation, March 8, 1862, Bock, *Tripartite Convention,* p. 480. Also see Cowley to Russell, March 14, 1862, extract in Lucia de Robina, *Reconciliacion de México y Francia, 1870-1880,* Archivo Histórico Diplomatico Mexicano, 2nd ser., no. 16 (México: Secretaría de Relaciones Exteriores, 1963), (hereinafter cited as AHDM), pp. 188-89; Russell to Wyke, March 15, 1862, Montluc, *Correspondance de Juárez et de Montluc,* VI, 338-40.

31. Thouvenel to minister of marine and colonies, June 12, 1861, cited by Bock, *Tripartite Convention,* p. 123; and minister of marine and colonies to Thouvenel, Paris, July 2, 1861, cited by ibid., p. 128.

The fate of Jecker and his claims, supported by the French government, stimulated great interest. When the Mexican government arrested the Swiss financier in 1862, ministers from Prussia to Peru had protested. Even the United States minister, evoking a reprimand from both President Abraham Lincoln and the Congress, unexpectedly interceded in his behalf.[32] The allied invasion of Mexico, however, exposed Jecker's claims to discerning scrutiny. Spanish, British, and French troops arrived in December 1861 and in January 1862.[33] At the first allied conference in Mexico on January 9, it was decided that each minister should prepare a list of reparations. At the second conference, Saligny expressed the impossibility of setting a specific amount and, as the other ministers were in a similar predicament, a mixed commission was proposed. Saligny opposed this suggested arbitration, and at the third conference on January 13 he set French claims at twelve million or two, either way, of the correct amount. When Saligny additionally demanded reimbursement of $15 million to Jecker, however, the Spanish and British commissioners declared this inadmissible.[34] At this time, in January 1862, Jecker was still a Swiss citizen; it was not until two months later, on March 26, that he was naturalized, with great haste, as a French citizen.[35] Disgusted with France, the British and the Spanish prepared to leave Mexico on April 9. Ten days later, a pronunciamiento in Córdoba proclaimed the French-supported Juan N. Almonte to be the supreme chief of

32. Letters on Jecker's behalf are in *House Ex. Doc.*, 37th Cong., 3rd sess., vol. 5, ser. 1161, doc. 23, pp. 3-27.

33. The Spanish fleet arrived December 14, 1861; the British and French fleets on January 6 and 7, 1862. Zamacois, *Historia de Méjico*, XV, 820-24. The Belgian minister reported the joint intervention as essential to restore order to Spanish America and to stop expansion of the United States. Further, he believed that most troops should be French and English commanded by a French general. T'Kint to de Vrière, December 28, 1861, AEB, CP, Mex., no. 47, and T'Kint to Rogier March 26, 1862, ibid., no. 59.

34. Matías Romero, *Historia de las intrigas europeas que ocasionaron la intervención francesa en México* (México: Imprenta del govierno, J. M. Sandoval, 1868), pp. 92-100; Francisco de Paula Arrangoiz [y Berzábal], *Méjico desde 1808 hasta 1867*, 4 vols. (Madrid: M. Rivadeneyra, 1871-72), II, 361, III, 20-21. Wyke to Russell, January 19, 1862, AHDM, pp. 141-46.

35. Kératry, *La créance Jecker*, pp. 18-19.

Mexico. In support of Almonte against Juárez, six thousand Frenchmen then turned toward Puebla.[36]

Jecker had served the French well by providing them with a pretext both for intervention and for a portion of Sonora. His 1856 surveying contract was of crucial importance to France. The Mexican government had granted one-half of its portion of Sonora's unclaimed land, as determined by the Jecker survey, to Antonio and Manuel Escandón, in exchange for construction of a railroad from Vera Cruz to Acapulco. This contract of April 5, 1861, had stipulated that the Escandón brothers would receive the titles to Sonoran property on completion of the line from Mexico City to Puebla. According to this grant by Juárez's government, the Escandóns could freely cede their rights to a third party. When the French arrived in Mexico in 1862, they significantly modified the contract: the Escandóns, cooperating with Napoleon, exchanged their rights to land in Sonora for cash payments and long-term bonds.[37] Having now obtained substantial concessions, the emperor needed another catalyst to organize and direct silver mining operations in Sonora. For this, he turned to an American, William McKendree Gwin.

---

36. Arrangoiz, *Méjico*, III, 69-70. During this fluid period of change in Mexico's government, the British opposed the idea of a monarchy for Mexico. See Russell to Cowley, September 9, 1861 and January 18, 1862. Britain, Public Record Office, Foreign Office (hereinafter PRO/FO), 519/199, Parts I and II. However, Drouyn de Lhuys was to remind Cowley that Queen Victoria had earlier looked favorably on Maximilian as a candidate for the Greek throne. Drouyn de Lhuys to Cowley, February 14, 1863, ibid., Part III, no. 153.

37. For the Escandóns' earlier connections with Jecker, Raousset-Boulbon, and Sonora, see Levasseur to minister of foreign affairs, April 27 and 30, 1853; Dano to minister of foreign affairs, July 18, 1853, September 1, 1853; Gabriac to minister of foreign affairs, December 31, 1854, June 26, 1857, Díaz, *Versión francesa de México*, I, 31-45; 55-58; 64-65; 157-59; 421-23; and Daniel Cosío Villegas, *Historia moderna de México*, 3 vols. (México: Editorial Hermes, 1955), II, *(La vida económica)*, 619-22. The French agreement with the Escandóns was signed December 23, 1862. Subsequent concessions by the empire to these brothers are in ibid., pp. 632-33.

William McKendree Gwin in the 1850s.
    (Daguerreotype at Library of Congress, Prints and Photographs
    Division—reproduction number LC USZ62-28283)

Napoleon III in 1863.
    (Portrait by Korean artist, based on Flandrin)

Chapter Six

William McKendree Gwin
Imperial Entrepreneur for Sonora

———— ◆ ————

William McKendree Gwin, had been one of California's first two senators, serving from 1849 to 1861. Sharing this distinction with John Charles Frémont, he had earlier (1841-1843) represented Mississippi in the House of Representatives. Since his property and investments happened to be primarily in the war-torn South, for him the Civil War became an enormous financial drain. With a goal of somehow restoring his personal wealth, in September of 1863 he moved to Paris.[1] Shortly after his arrival he was received in private audience at the Tuileries by invitation of Napoleon III, and at this first meeting the emperor directed their discussion to detailed military and geological maps of Sonora.[2]

Gwin's rapid entrance into the social, political, and economic life of the Second Empire had begun at the home of his friend and fellow exile, William W. Corcoran, a prominent Washington banker who had already established himself in Parisian society. While senator, Gwin had previously met the Marquis de Montholon, former French consul in New York. Through Corcoran he renewed this acquaintanceship, except that now Montholon had just been appointed minister to Mexico.[3]

---

1. Gwin to his brother, June 1, 1864, Coleman, "Gwin's Plan" *Overland Monthly,* 18 (August 1891): 205. Trained in both law and medicine, Gwin successfully practiced the latter for six years. See William McKendree Gwin, "Memoirs of Hon. William M. Gwin," William Henry Ellison, ed., *California Historical Society Quarterly,* 19 (March, 1940): 1
2. Coleman, "Gwin's Plan," *Overland Monthly* 17 (May 1891): 497, citing J. F. H. Claiborne, *Mississippi as a Province, Territory and State* (Jackson, Miss., 1880).
3. Gwin had, of course, been strongly opposed to French activities in Sonora in the 1850s. For his protests, see *Congressional Globe,* Cong., 2nd sess., appendix, pp. 100, 130-33, 146.

When conversation turned to Mexico, Montholon, aware of Gwin's experience with California mining problems and intrigued by his knowledge of Sonora, realized that this American would be of interest to Napoleon.[4] Accordingly, he met again with Gwin the following day. On this occasion they expanded their discussion of the previous evening to include potential development plans for northern Mexico's mineral resources.[5] Montholon then arranged further influential contacts for Gwin. Within a month after his arrival, Gwin had received invitations from the Emperor Napoleon III and the Duc de Morny, the emperor's half-brother and president of the *corps législatif.* By the end of 1863, Napoleon had introduced Gwin to his finance minister, Achille Fould, and to his minister of foreign affairs, Drouyn de Lhuys.[6]

The French had been interested in Mexican silver and Sonoran mines in particular well before Gwin arrived in Paris.[7] On May 27, 1863, only ten days after the capture of Puebla, General Elie Frédéric Forey prohibited all exportation of gold or silver from Mexico.[8] A few days later Alphonse Lamartine was explaining to Emile Ollivier that the expedition to Mexico was justified by the "incalculable riches" of Sonora's mines.[9] Balancing this optimism Lord John Russell caustically observed that it would "still cost many a hard dollar before the mines

---

4. Gwin's latest biographer states that Gwin also talked with Baron Henri Mercier, French minister to the United States, within a few days after his initial talk with Montholon. However, Mercier was in Washington at this time and did not return to France until December 1863. Thomas, *Between Two Empires,* p. 293.

5. McPherson, *William McKendrie Gwin,* pp. 252-53. While imprisoned at Fort Jackson after the Civil War, Gwin alleged that Montholon, then French minister to the United States, was "entirely responsible" for his (Gwin's) participation in Napoleon's enterprise. Gwin to Montholon, October 15, 1865, Coleman, "Gwin's Plan," *Overland Monthly* 18 (August 1891): 209.

6. Ibid., 17 (May 1891): 497-501 and 18 (August 1891): 212.

7. Thomas mistakenly credits Gwin with initiating French interest in Sonora. Thomas, *Between Two Empires,* p. 289. French officials, however, had made the initial contacts with Gwin, who then prepared his mining and colonization plans for Sonora at their request. Gwin, "Memoirs" 19 (June 1940): 178.

8. José Sebastián Seguara, ed., *Boletín de las leyes del Imperio mexicano ó sea Código de la restauración,* 4 vols. (México: Imprenta literaria, 1863-65), I, 28-29; 283-84. Forey made this announcement, in effect until September 7, 1863, on the advice of M. Budin, intendant of finances, sent to Mexico by Napoleon.

9. Emile Ollivier, *La intervención francesa y el imperio de Maximiliano en México,* 2nd ed. (México: Ediciones Centenario, 1963), p. 101. This conversation centered on French election results of May 30-31, 1863

are quietly in the possession of France."10 Even before the occupation of Mexico City in June 1863 the French ministry of agriculture, commerce, and public works had sent a M. Laur to Sonora for a detailed report of mineral wealth there.11 Timing seemed important in the spring and summer of 1863. Before and during the months Laur was in Sonora, European ministries heard reports that President Juárez was willing to sell northern Mexican provinces to the United States.12 Supplementing Laur's study, the French minister of public instruction appointed another commission in 1863 to make a scientific expedition into Sonora. In early 1864 this second commission submitted to the emperor a heartening report on the mineral wealth of that state.13

These candid inquiries were coupled with indirect means to acquire the mineral rights of Sonora. In August 1863 the French foreign minister delineated the "direct interest" France had in Mexican finances. Forthrightly stating, "We have the right to exercise an active fiscal influence upon the administration of the finances," Drouyn de Lhuys specified that special French agents, delegated by the minister of finance, would facilitate the reorganization of Mexican finances. They took charge of customs collections and their financiers took over Mexico's treasury department. An "indisputable" commission, instituted under the French ministry of foreign affairs, was to settle all claims. Drouyn de Lhuys now mentioned a significant second set of claims, based on military expenses incurred by the expedition. These military costs, to be reimbursed by the French-sponsored

---

10. Russell to Cowley, June 13, 1863. PRO/FO, 519/200, part I, no. 134.

11. Charles Blanchot, *Mémoires, L'Intervention Française au Mexique*, 3 vols. (Paris: Emile Nourry, 1911), II, 254. Laur stopped his explorations in October 1863 because of Apache raids. Bazaine to Napoleon III, October 26, 1863, Bazaine Archives, vol. I, f. 183.

12. Juárez was particularly perturbed that this assertion was made by Leopoldo O'Donnell, president of the council of ministers of the Spanish government, in his reply to the speech of the crown. Juárez to the editor of the *Diario,* February 22, 1863, *House Ex. Doc.,* 39th Cong. 1st sess., vol. 1, pt. 3, ser 1246, doc. 1, p. 496.

13. Article 4, Document from Minister of Finance, Paris, February 25, 1864, concerning Finances of Mexico, in HHUSA, Max., box 33, fasc. 17, pt. 2, doc. 8. This report is in *Archives de la commission scientifique du Mexique* (Paris, 1864-65), a copy of which was in Maximilian's personal library, according to Count Egon Caesar Corti, *Maximilian and Charlotte of Mexico,* 2 vols. (New York: Alfred A. Knopf, 1929), II, 960.

Mexican government, constituted a further basis for Napoleon's attempt to obtain mineral rights in Sonora.[14] By September 1863 when Gwin arrived in Paris, the French were already poised to invade Sonora.

Although specific dates are frustratingly missing from Gwin's memoirs and letters, he had arrived in Paris "early" in September.[15] French moves before his arrival, his early reception by the emperor, and the rapid events of September 1863 indicate that Napoleon was already prepared to implement direct steps to obtain Sonora's silver wealth.[16] He had now found the leader capable of directing the mineral development of Sonora—hopefully to parallel or exceed the spectacular wealth of California.[17] After being introduced to Gwin by the emperor, the finance minister met him for two interviews, and then asked him to submit specific mining plans to the minister of foreign affairs. These proposals were adopted at a meeting of the Council of State, over which the emperor presided. Napoleon then requested that Gwin prepare an additional memorandum for Austria's archduke, Maximilian von Hapsburg.[18]

Gwin's mining plans for Sonora revealed audacity and practicality. While his frontier bluntness had appealed to a Bonaparte, his lack of finesse appalled a Hapsburg. Gwin informed Maximilian that his own

14. Drouyn de Lhuys to Bazaine, August 17, 1863, *La Sociedad,* n.d., pp. 1-2, enclosed in a dispatch from Corwin to Seward, December 26, 1863, NA, State, MD Mex., vol. 30, microcopy 97, roll 32

15. Thomas, *Between Two Empires,* p. 279.

16. Corti, *Maximilian and Charlotte,* I, 326-27, erroneously states that Gwin drew Napoleon's attention to Sonora's mines. Napoleon's interest in the silver of Sonora substantially antedated Gwin's arrival in Paris.

17. Gustave Léon Niox, *L'Expédition du Mexique, 1861-67. Récit politique et militaire* (Paris: Librairie militaire de J. Dumoine, 1874), p. 503. Napoleon's judgment of Gwin's mining and business ability was later proven sound. In 1868, after returning to California from France, Gwin purchased and revitalized a neglected gold mine in Calaveras County. Within two years it yielded from $15,000 to $20,000 per month in gold bullion and, for some decades, it continued to be one of California's largest gold-producing mines. Thomas, *Between Two Empires,* 368-73.

18. McPherson, *William McKendree Gwin,* p. 254; and "Memorandum from Gwin to Maxmilian," Coleman, "Gwin's Plan," *Overland Monthly* 17 (May 1891): 499-501. Thomas is in error when he states that Gwin presented the memorandum directly to Maximilian while the archduke was in Paris in September 1863. Thomas, *Between Two Empires,* p. 298. Maxmilian was not in Paris until March 1864, and Gwin's first interview with him was at that time.

interest in northern Mexico stemmed from his senatorial days when he was instrumental in creating the territory of Arizona and in framing the boundary portion of the Gadsden Treaty, which ceded Mexican territory to the United States. During these investigations he had discovered valuable, but idle, silver mines in Sonora and Chihuahua.[19]

Disregarding European wariness about the expansionist tendencies of the United States, Gwin explained the details of a Sonoran surveying contract in the late 1850s between "certain parties" and the central Mexican government. These parties included Jean Baptiste Jecker. As noted earlier, Captain Isham had engaged Captains Whiting and Stone, United States army engineers, as leaders of the surveying expedition.[20] A portion of the lands surveyed were to be granted to the surveying company in payment for its services, but Indians and Sonoran authorities had expelled the surveyors. In 1859 Captains Whiting and Stone, claiming Sonora's mineral wealth was superior to California, petitioned Gwin to seek United States protection to enable them to complete their survey and recoup their expenditures.[21]

Gwin had recommended the officers to President Buchanan, who, convinced that the rights of United States citizens had been violated, directed the secretary of war to send General Winfield Scott to Sonora with one thousand dragoons and artillery. However, there was more involved than the mere fulfillment of a contract. Captain Stone

---

19. Gwin to Maximilian, September 1863, Coleman, "Gwin's Plan," *Overland Monthly* 17 (May 1891): 499-501. Ironically, Juan Nepumoceno Almonte, grand marshal of Maximilian's court and later his minister to France, had been the Mexican minister assigned the painful task of working with Gwin and Senator Thomas Jefferson Rusk of Texas in the severance of this land from Mexico. Almonte was understandably hostile to Gwin throughout the empire. Ibid., 514. Actually, Gwin had favored United States expansion southward since 1846. *Congressional Globe,* 33rd Cong., 1st sess., pp. 206-10, 882; and Gwin, "Memoirs," 19 (June, 1940), 177-78.

20. Coleman, "Gwin's Plan," *Overland Monthly* 17 (May 1891): 499; and McPherson, *William McKendree Gwin,* p. 252, citing *San Francisco Bulletin,* November 19, 1859.

21. Gwin to Maximilian, September, 1863, Coleman, "Gwin's Plan," *Overland Monthly* 17 (May 1891): 500. For Gwin's cooperative part in a resolution offered by Senator Sam Houston concerning the establishment of a protectorate over Mexico and Central American states, see *Congressional Globe,* 35th Cong., 1st sess., pp. 735-36; and *Senate Journal,* 35th Cong., 1st sess., ser. 917, pp. 198, 362, 583.

urged using this military contingent as the nucleus for a mining settlement to attract thousands of miners, subdue the Indians, and cause Sonora to increase in population as rapidly as California. The rationale was that the United States, bound under the Gadsden Treaty to protect Mexico against wild Indian tribes, could best meet this obligation by establishing a large population in Sonora.[22] However, twenty-four hours after President Buchanan gave these orders, he revoked them. Denouncing Buchanan's "vacillating policy", Gwin had then become a supporter of Napoleon's Sonoran plans, which would "accomplish more important results."[23]

At this point, Maximilian must have been dubious as to any altruistic role Gwin might play in Mexico. But Gwin hastily detailed the services he could render Maximilian and Mexico. The vulnerability of the northern Mexican border to marauding bands of Indians and "the more dangerous designs of an adjacent turbulent and aggressive government" could be ameliorated by populating this area with loyal imperialists who would create a secure frontier. He claimed that Sonora's rich mineral deposits would attract thousands of miners if immigrants were assured of initial military protection. Gwin pointed out various mining bonanzas in the United States which, within a few months, had brought large numbers of miners to previously desolate

---

22. Gwin to Maximilian, September 1863, Coleman, "Gwin's Plan," *Overland Monthly* 17 (May 1891): 500. Gwin is probably referring here to article 11 of the Treaty of Guadalupe Hidalgo which was revoked by article 2 of the Gadsden Treaty. For the Treaty of Guadalupe Hidalgo, see U.S., *Statutes at Large*, vol. 9, pt. 2 (December 1845-March 1851), "Treaty of Peace, Friendship, Limits, and Settlement with the Republic of Mexico," February 2, 1848, art. 11, p. 930. For the Gadsden Treaty, see U.S., *Statutes at Large*, vol. 10, pt. 2 (December 1851-March 1855), "Treaty with Mexico," December 30, 1853, art. 2, p. 1033. Captain Charles Stone resided in Sonora during 1858-59 and reported on the agricultural and mineral resources of the area, as well as giving details on the specific Indian tribes creating problems. See his "Notes on the State of Sonora," *The Historical Magazine*, V (June 1861): 161-69. For another good view of chronic instability due to civil war and to Indian unrest and raids in 1859, see Carlota Miles, ed. and trans., *Almada of Alamos: The Diary of Don Bartholome* (Tucson, Arizona Silhouettes, 1962), pp. 36-37, 40-45, 47-52, 55-58.
23. Gwin to Maximilian, September 1863, Coleman, "Gwin's Plan", *Overland Monthly* 17 (May 1891): 500; and Evan J. Coleman, "Dr. Gwin and Judge Black on Buchanan," *Overland Monthly* 19 (January 1892): 87-92.

areas. He particularly stressed California's population increase from 15,000 in 1849 to more than 500,000 by 1861, and the inference was clear that his political experience during those dramatic twelve years would be a most valuable asset for the new empire.[24]

Gwin requested no personal concessions in this memorandum. His objectives appear to have been three-fold: as a former United States senator, to relate his familiarity with Mexico; to impress Maximilian of the latent mineral value of Sonora; and to emphasize the benefits, and necessity, of populating Mexico's northern frontier. However, to the Austrian archduke with European apprehensions concerning United States aggrandizement, Gwin's acknowledgment of earlier participation in divesting Mexico of territory made him uncomfortable and alarmed. When José María Gutiérrez de Estrada, a Mexican monarchist in Rome, wrote that many Confederates had sentiments favorable to a monarchy, the archduke firmly noted in the margin of the letter, "They have always been, and will always be, the sworn adversaries of Mexico whatever the form of its government."[25] When Gutiérrez commented that Gwin was "a real pioneer," Maximilian countered, "Yes! A pioneer for the South!"[26]

---

24. Gwin to Maximilian, September 1863, Coleman, "Gwin's Plan," *Overland Monthly* 17 (May 1891): 501. Gwin had a valid argument. Two months later, on November 20, 1863, Seward inquired of Matías Romero, Juárez's minister to the United States, about the authority of General José Domingo Cortés, a Spaniard who presented himself to Seward as the representative of Sonora, Sinaloa, Chihuahua, and Durango. Cortés had solicited Seward for these states to be annexed to the United States, but Romero assured Seward that Cortés was an "intriguer" who had no authority to make such an offer. Romero to Seward, July 9, 1864, referring to this November 20, 1863 conference with Seward, with enclosures from Luis Terrazas, Chihuahua, January 11, 1864, and F. García Morales, Sinaloa, January 24, 1864; Seward to Romero, July 15, 1864, *House Ex. Doc.,* 39th Cong., 1st sess., vol. 1, pt. 3, ser. 1246, doc. 1, pp. 576-78.

25. Daniel Dawson, *The Mexican Adventure* (London: G. Bell & Sons Ltd., 1935), pp. 335-36, citing letters in HHUSA, Max., Gutiérrez to Baron de Pont, October 24, November 18, December 31, 1863; and Gwin to Gutiérrez, memorandum, October 1863.

26. Ibid. Gutiérrez's tentative support of both the Confederates and Gwin did not jeopardize his relations with Maximilian. Gutiérrez de Estrada to Manuel Larrainzai, Paris, January 10, 1864, Maximilian and Carlota Collection, Rare Book Room, box 5, Fondren Library, Rice University, Houston, Texas. Gwin was to remain suspect in Maximilian's eyes. See Dano to Drouyn de Lhuys, June 11, 1864, France, Archives du ministère des affaires étrangères, Correspondance Politique (hereinafter cited as AEF,CP), Mex., vol. 63.

While the Mexican press editorialized, "The greed which not only our neighboring enemies but other foreigners have for Sonora is not new," the French emperor moved to acquire Sonora's mineral rights.[27] In February 1864, the Marquis de Montholon, now French minister to Mexico, concluded a convention with the Mexican Council of Regency which placed Sonora under the "direct and sovereign protection" of France for fifteen years. France was to be granted all rights of prospecting for metals and, in return, a 10 percent royalty on the net proceeds would be given to the Mexican treasury.[28] This convention, ostensibly designed to pay Mexico's debts to France, particularly stressed expenses incurred by the military expedition.[29] Although no territory was actually ceded, Maximilian adamantly opposed this action of the Regency.[30] He likewise unequivocally

27. Hanna, "Immigration Movement," p. 238, quoting *El Cronista,* January 22, 1864.

28. "Convención de 1864," signed by the Marquis de Montholon, José Miguel Arroyo, and M. Castillo, February 17, 1864, HHUSA, Max., box 140. While the convention included only Sonora, there were later plans to form companies between both empires that would also regenerate mines in Lower California, Sinaloa, Chihuahua, and Durango to meet Mexico's obligations. Vela Leatrice Lynn, *The Political Career of Teodosio Lares, 1848-1867* (Ph.D. diss., University of Texas, 1951), pp. 270-71.

29. This is alluded to in the letter of August 17, 1863, from Drouyn de Lhuys to Bazaine before Gwin ever arrived in Paris, NA, State, MD Mex., microcopy 97, roll 31, vol. 30.

30. Shortly after Maximilian's arrival in Mexico, he dismissed José Miguel Arroyo, undersecretary of state for the Regency, who had concluded the convention with Montholon. Corti, *Maximilian,* II, 426-27; and Blanchot, *L'Intervention Française,* II, 255. Lefèvre, a political opponent of Napoleon and an adherent of the Mexican Republican Government, stated that Napoleon insisted on inclusion of an article in the Treaty of Miramar which would ratify all acts of the Regency, in order to guarantee French sovereignty over Sonora. Maximilian, declaring he would not accept the Mexican crown under such conditions, refused to accept this proposed clause. Lefèvre, *Documents officiels,* II, 91-92. For an analysis of how this convention affected the personal relations between Montholon and Maximilian, see Blondeel to Rogier, February 27, 1865 AEB, CP, Mex., vol. 1, no. 69. For more on this convention, subsequent financial negotiations, secret articles, bonds and loans, see Arnold Blumberg, *The Diplomacy of the Mexican Empire 1863-1867* (Philadelphia, American Philosophical Society, 1971), pp. 11-14.

rejected a draft of the proposed treaty that included cession of Sonora's mineral rights to France. His recalcitrance on the issue paid off when he was able to accept the final Treaty of Miramar in which Sonora was not even mentioned.[31]

Plans for Sonora continued in Paris. At the request of the French minister of foreign affairs, Gwin submitted a new memorandum to Napoleon on January 5, 1864. Correctly surmising that the success of his mining project depended on the French emperor's support, he emphasized the advantage to both France and Mexico if "one of the richest" mineral areas in America were developed. Referring to a previous interview with Napoleon, Gwin requested a small military force to protect early immigrants from Indian depredations. Gwin's plan required Maximilian's approval to enter Sonora and Napoleon's military aid to subdue the Indians. Consistently pointing to immense financial and commercial benefits, Gwin claimed that royalties from mining concessions and customs revenue from supplies for new settlers would enable Maximilian to pay the debt to France while alleviating the entire indebtedness of the Mexican empire.[32] Later in 1864 he was more specific, as perhaps he was in personal conversation during these first months of negotiation, about his role in the unprecedented growth and wealth of California.[33] His former political stature there, he asserted, would provide confidence in the stability of Sonora's development which would attract miners from the United States. While Gwin presented his proposals, French engineers were submitting mining surveys of Sonora substantiating claims of its great mineral wealth.[34]

In March of 1864, again at the request of the French minister of foreign affairs, Gwin prepared for Napoleon extended plans to develop

---

31. See article 5 of the "Projet de convention pour le maintien d'un corps auxiliaire français au Mexique," February 10, 1864, HHUSA, Max., box 12. See also Stout, *Liberators*, p. 175.
32. Gwin to Napoleon III, January 5, 1864, Coleman, "Gwin's Plan," *Overland Monthly* 17 (May 1891): 501-02.
33. "Memorandum Accompanying the Project of a Treaty Giving a Concession of the Mines of North Mexico to France," ibid., 511-12.
34. Gwin to Napoleon III, January 5, 1864, ibid., 502; Article 4, Document from Minister of Finance, Paris, February 25, 1864, concerning Finances of Mexico, HHUSA, Max., box 33, fasc. 17, pt. 2, doc. 8.

western Chihuahua in addition to Sonora.[35] Baron Henri Mercier, former French minister to the United States and Gwin's acquaintance since the 1850s when they were both in Washington, took these plans to Drouyn de Lhuys, who presented them to the French emperor. They were next submitted, through the Mexican minister to France, José Manuel Hidalgo, to Maximilian, then in Paris working out details of the Treaty of Miramar with Napoleon. Maximilian invited Gwin to the Tuileries and, according to Gwin, he approved and supported the proposals.[36]

These new plans drawn up by Gwin would create a yet unnamed military department that would include the eastern portion of Sonora and the western portion of Chihuahua, with boundaries carefully drawn to avoid lands already occupied. This largely uninhabited area would be declared imperial domain, open to settlement, and all mining claims not occupied and worked at the date of the projected decree would be open to "the first comers."[37] The Mexican treasury would receive 6 percent, paid in bullion, of the gross proceeds of all the gold and silver mines.[38]

Drawing on his California experiences, Gwin assured honest reports and receipts by the establishment of military protection, government

---

35. "Note by Gwin," Coleman, "Gwin's Plan," *Overland Monthly* 17 (May 1891): 497, 503-05. At this same time, March 1864, Roger Dubos, French vice-consul in Chihuahua, made favorable reports on the great mineral wealth of Chihuahua. Roger Dubos, "Notice sur les Mines de l'Etat de Chihuahua," doc. 19414, cited by Luis Weckmann, *Las relaciones franco-mexicanas,* 2 vols. (México: Secretaría de relaciones exteriores, 1961-62), II, 319-20.

36. "Note by Gwin," Coleman, "Gwin's Plan," *Overland Monthly* 17 (May 1891): 497, 502; and doc. 19417, March 1864, M. Gwin, "Exposé d'un plan de colonisation dans les Etats de Sonora et Chihuahua," cited by Weckmann, *Las relaciones franco-mexicanas,* II, 320-21. Maximilian's apparent duplicity may be seen in his refusal, at this very time, to include a cession of Sonora's mineral rights to France in the Treaty of Miramar.

37. Gwin's "Plan of Colonization in Sonora and Chihuahua," and "Notes Explanatory of the Plan of Colonization in Sonora and Chihuahua," Paris, March 1864, Coleman, "Gwin's Plan," *Overland Monthly* 17 (May 1891): 502-03. Gwin's plan was based on Spanish mining laws which put a premium on free access to mining opportunities. See Blondeel to Rogier, Feb. 27, 1865, AEB,CP, Mex., vol. 1, no. 69.

38. Note the contrast here with the Montholon-Regency Treaty, mentioned above, which provided for 10 percent of the net proceeds for the Mexican treasury.

assay offices, and reduction works. He proposed that a tribunal, appointed by Maximilian, be established to adjudicate previous mine claims which, if found valid, would be financially reimbursed from the imperial treasury, thus avoiding costly litigation for miners. Gwin interestingly concluded, "All grants of land or mining privileges which have been made within the boundaries of said Department since the landing at Vera Cruz of the joint 'Army of Occupation' of France, England, and Spain, to be declared null and void."[39]

Rewording Stone's 1859 request for United States military protection, Gwin suggested that the French army provide a thousand mounted men and a battery of mountain howitzers to protect miners against both Indian depredations and any "desperate characters" infiltrating among honest immigrants. He insisted that these French soldiers be the best in Mexico, and he proposed that the proceeds of mines assigned to the military be divided pro rata, according to rank. "They would all in that event come away rich at the end of their service." Gwin carefully weighed routes and timing of military marches to coincide with the July rainy season, thus providing food and water for horses and men, and enabling engineers to build dams for mining operations during the dry season.

Aware of the vulnerability of Mexico, Gwin insisted that miners coming from Canada, France, Germany, Spain, South America, and the United States would furnish vital support for Maximilian. Following an interview with Baron Mercier on March 12, 1864, Gwin alluded to the uneasiness of Napoleon and Maximilian about American designs, admitting "I do not deny that at present there is danger of Sonora being lost to the Mexican Crown. It is entirely destitute of protection,—a waif floating about, to be picked up by the first comers."[40] Juan N. Almonte, president of the Regency, had also reminded Maximilian about the susceptibility of this region.[41] In

---

39. Gwin's "Plan of Colonization in Sonora and Chihuahua," and "Notes Explanatory of the Plan of Colonization in Sonora and Chihuahua," Paris, March 1864, ibid., 502-05.
40. Gwin to Mercier, March 12, 1864, ibid., 505.
41. Almonte to Maximilian, November 27, 1863, Mexico, Almonte correspondence, 1862-66, from HHUSA, Max., copies in the Barker Library, University of Texas.

Paris John Bigelow had fulsome praise for the French role in Mexico, writing that her success there "will rank among the greatest glories of the Second Empire."[42]

In March 1864 both France and the United States were aware that Sonora and other northern states were nominally controlled by Juárez. Napoleon ordered French troops to Sonora, ostensibly to counter California emigrants reported to have landed at Guaymas to claim land grants made by the Mexican president. The French chargé d'affaires to the United States, Louis de Geoffroy, heatedly protested these concessions from Juárez. Seward replied that while he appreciated such "frankness," he had no knowledge of such an emigration, and he assured Geoffroy that the United States would maintain its neutrality.[43] Meanwhile, on March 28, Napoleon sent General Charles Auguste de Frossard, his aide-de-camp and inspector-general of artillery, to Miramar to obtain Maximilian's acquiescence of French control in Sonora; but Maximilian refused to commit himself.[44] On April 14, 1864, his imperial ship left Trieste for Mexico. Two emperors were now deeply involved in the fate of Sonora's mineral wealth.

As the French moved towards Sonora, they pressured the Mexican minister in Paris to obtain Maximilian's approval. José Manuel Hidalgo, the most influential Mexican in France, had been instrumental in both encouraging the intervention and in the selection of Maximilian. Now in the uncomfortable position of trying to placate both emperors, Hidalgo wrote the Mexican foreign minister that he had pointed out to the French foreign minister the highly delicate nature of Gwin's plans for Sonora, because of the precedent set by

---

42. Bigelow to Chevalier, March 8, 1864, John Bigelow Papers, box 1, New York Public Library.

43. Corwin to Seward, March 28, 1864, NA, State, MD Mex., microcopy 97, roll 31, vol. 30; Louis de Geoffroy to Seward, Washington, April 3, 1864; and Seward to Geoffroy, Washington, April 6, 1864. The last two letters both in *House Ex. Doc.*, 39th Cong., 1st sess., vol. 1, pt. 3, ser. 1246, doc. 1, pp. 723-24.

44. Corti, *Maximilian*, I, 327, 339-41; Suzanne Desternes and Henriette Chandet, *Maximilien et Charlotte* (Paris: Librairie Academique Perrin, 1964), p. 191; and Maximilian to Napoleon III, April 8, 1864, Corti, *Maximilian*, I, 402.

American colonists in Texas.[45] Then Hidalgo perfunctorily forwarded Gwin's French-supported proposals to Maximilian.

Amidst the complex issues spinning off from the American Civil War, Hidalgo feared Southern intrigues in Sonora, in spite of his sympathy for the Confederate cause.[46] Maximilian's Mexican minister in Brussels, Francisco de Paula Arrangoiz, a reactionary and former republican finance minister, was aware of Hidalgo's communications with Maximilian, and mistakenly castigated Gwin as the "active agent" responsible for sundering California from Mexico.[47] Relatively free from the steady pressure of French support for Gwin, Arrangoiz portrayed the senator as a man of no principle who planned to unite Sonora, Sinaloa, California, and Oregon in an independent republic. Hidalgo was equally but more subtly alarmed.[48] He informed his new emperor that while Drouyn de Lhuys insisted on a "prompt resolution" of French plans for Sonora, he would dutifully await Maximilian's instructions.[49]

Two weeks later Hidalgo revealed intense French pressure for Mexican acceptance of Gwin's plans. Mercier, now reassigned to Madrid,

---

45. José Manuel Hidalgo, "Notes secrètes de M. Hidalgo à développer le jour où il conviendra d'écrire l'histoire de la fondation de l'empire mexicain", HHUSA, Max., box 19, no. 46; Hidalgo to J. M. Arroyo, April 29, 1864, doc. 19415, cited by Weckmann, *Las relaciones franco mexicanas,* II, 320; and Hidalgo to J. M. Arroyo, May 14, 1864, doc. 19420, ibid., 321.

46. Hidalgo to Maximilian, April 30, 1864, HHUSA, Max., box 19, pt. 2, pp. 264-65.

47. Francisco de Paula Arrangoiz to Maximilian, April 30, 1864, ibid., box 18, konvolut A, docs. 18-19. The bitterness of Mexicans toward Californians is understandable, considering the filibustering attempts emanating from that state in the 1850s. When William Walker proclaimed Lower California a republic, a California editor prematurely exulted, "Another star is added to the bright Anglo-Saxon constellation. Another sovereign state is knocking for admission into the American Union." *Alta California,* December 8, 1853, quoted by McPherson, *William McKendree Gwin,* p. 247.

48. Arrangoiz to Maximilian, Paris, April 30, 1864, HHUSA, Max., box 18, konvolut A, docs. 18-19. Unfortunately, the Austrian penchant for codes is introduced into these diplomatic letters during this period and many lines, undoubtedly significant, consist of numbers. Hidalgo to Arroyo, Paris, April 30, 1864, Lefèvre, *Documents officiels,* II, 94. Arroyo forwarded Gwin's plan to the minister of development (Fomento) and asked him for a report. Arroyo to Hidalgo, June 15, 1864, ibid., p. 96. For the role of Arrangoiz during this period, see Blumberg, *Diplomacy of the Mexican Empire,* pp. 20-21, 44.

49. Hidalgo to Maximilian, April 30, 1864, HHUSA, Max., box 19, pt. 2, p. 265.

and Drouyn de Lhuys continued their steady insistence that Maximilian comply with French wishes. Hidalgo, distressed that negotiations about Sonora had escalated to occupy most of his time as Mexican minister to France, urged Maximilian to evaluate Gwin's proposals.[50] A year later the charge was made against Hidalgo that he represented French interests more than Mexican.[51] While there is certainly some truth in this judgment, Hidalgo seemed most of all to simply want the Sonoran issue resolved. He cynically repeated news from the United States that Gwin would supposedly become "the Duke of Sonora"—an emotional accusation that he realized would negatively influence the former archduke of Austria. At the same time, Gwin's protests to the French foreign minister that Hidalgo had not forwarded his proposals on to the Mexican emperor disturbed him. Almost plaintively, Hidalgo begged Maximilian to consider his previous dispatches on Sonora and to consult with Roger Dubos, French vice-consul in Chihuahua, whom he recommended as an "honorable and intelligent" man.[52] Failing to please either the Mexican or French court, Hidalgo eventually incurred the wrath of both.

At this time, in the winter and spring of 1863-64, Lincoln and Seward, uneasy about French supplies to the Confederate navy, assiduously avoided confrontations with France.[53] However, on April 4, 1864, the United States Congress passed a resolution protesting the "deplorable events transpiring in Mexico," causing Drouyn de Lhuys to ask Dayton bluntly, "Do you bring us peace or bring us war?"[54] Seward, aware that this was not the time for "idle menaces" to Napoleon, believed there was no need to "gasconade about Mexico when we are in a struggle for our own life."[55] Thus the French continued their false hopes for United States neutrality.

---

50. Hidalgo to Maximilian, May 15, 1864, ibid., pp. 281-82.

51. Corti, *Maximilian*, II, 518.

52. Hidalgo to Maximilian, May 15, 1864, HHUSA, Max., box 19, pt. 2, pp. 281-82.

53. White, *American Opinion of France*, p. 157.

54. *Congressional Globe*, 38th Cong., 1st sess., pp. 1408, 2475.

55. Seward to Bigelow, May 21, 1864, quoted by Samuel Flagg Bemis, ed., *The American Secretaries of State and Their Diplomacy* 10 vols., (New York: Alfred A. Knopf, 1928), VII, 107. For Seward's ideas that the U.S. would "grow naturally," informally absorbing nearby areas, in the context of a study of a variety of U.S. schemes for business ventures and concessions in Mexico, see Thomas Schoonover, "U.S. Economic Penetration into Mexico in the 1860s," paper presented at the Missouri Valley History Conference (1978) at Omaha.

On June 1, 1864, a month and a half after Emperor Maximilian left Trieste for Mexico, William McKendree Gwin, buoyant with hope, left Southampton, also heading for Mexico.[56] During the nine months since he had arrived in France, there had been frequent interviews with the Duc de Morny, two of them in the month before his departure.[57] Confessing that his former ambitions had been for political power, Gwin admitted that he was now seeking only personal wealth. A hesitancy concerning future obstacles, especially Mexican prejudice against Americans, was interspersed with confidence that two emperors supported him. Gwin had also recognized the nationalism that would, indeed, defeat him, but erroneously believed that Maximilian favored his plan for Sonora.[58]

Gwin's departure for Mexico caused a flurry of diplomatic letters. John Slidell, Confederate commissioner to France, informed Judah P. Benjamin, Confederate secretary of state, that Napoleon had directed General Achille François Bazaine to help Gwin. According to Gwin, General Bazaine considered the emperor's written instructions "a positive order" to establish him in Sonora.[59] Although Napoleon had advised Gwin to disassociate himself from Southerners, Slidell apparently thought Gwin's project, approved by the French emperor, would help the Confederacy.[60] The governor of California, Frederick F. Low, informed Seward that France, requiring indemnity for military expenditures, would demand and receive both Sonora and Sinaloa. Gwin, Low stated, had been sent as Napoleon's emissary to conclude these negotiations.[61] Continuing to act in accordance with

56. Blattner, "Political Career of Gwin," p. 112.
57. Morny to Gwin, May 4 and 26, 1864; Coleman, "Gwin's Plan," *Overland Monthly* 18 (August 1891): 205.
58. Gwin to his brother, June 1, 1864, ibid., 206.
59. Slidell to Benjamin, Paris, June 2, 1864, John Bigelow, *Retrospections of an Active Life,* 3 vols. (New York: Baker & Taylor Co., 1909), II, 190; and Gwin to his son, July 27, 1864, Coleman, "Gwin's Plan," *Overland Monthly* 18 (August 1891): 204.
60. J. Fred Rippy, "Mexican Projects of the Confederates," *Southwestern Historical Quarterly* 22 (April 1919): 314; and Slidell to Benjamin, June 2, 1864, Bigelow, *Retrospections,* II, 190. Slidell had been at Corcoran's home when Gwin and Montholon first discussed Sonora.
61. Low to Seward, July 18, 1864; and Seward to Dayton, August 18, 1864, *Senate Ex. Doc.,* 38th Cong., 2nd sess., vol. 1, ser. 1209, doc. 11, pp. 136-37.

his previous statement, Seward maintained that the spring campaigns "abate the interest with which we have been watching the commotions of Europe."[62]

Thomas Corwin, United States minister to Mexico, also knew about Gwin's impending arrival and the purpose of his mission. Recounting Maximilian's aloofness toward Gwin, Corwin interpreted the Mexican emperor's reluctance to participate in the project as fear of alienating the United States over any demonstration of sympathy with Confederates.[63] On the same day that Corwin wrote to Seward, William Preston, Confederate envoy to Mexico, wrote to his president, Jefferson Davis, revealing some interesting sidelights which had occurred in Paris. Preston related a dispute between Gwin and Fould, French finance minister, concerning Sonora. Fould had proposed that large mining monopolies be given to French corporations for the development of Sonora; but, to his annoyance, Napoleon endorsed Gwin's plan based on individual entrepreneurs instead of on corporate wealth. Mistakenly asserting that Maximilian approved Gwin's project, Preston expected that Gwin would be appointed superintendent or governor of Sonora.[64]

In an atmosphere of international intrigue, Gwin arrived in Mexico on July 1, 1864.[65] He soon found himself embroiled in three sets of factional feuds: the Union vs. the Confederacy, Juárez vs. Maximilian, and Mexico vs. France. Unfortunately for Gwin, he cast his lot—in all three cases—with the losers.

Gwin's buoyancy was deflated during the frustrating months after his arrival, as he quickly became involved in the Franco-Mexican dispute. His first problem was the inability to meet openly with General

---

62. Seward to James S. Pike, May 6, 1864, ibid., pt. 3, p. 314.

63. Corwin to Seward, June 18, 1864, NA, State, MD Mex., microcopy 97, roll 31, vol. 30. Barely three weeks later Seward received from Romero a copy of *La Accion*, no. 28 published at Saltillo on June 18, 1864. This contained a penetrating article by Francisco Zarco, formerly secretary of foreign relations under Juarez. The article was a critical economic analysis showing the virtual impossibility for the new empire to enjoy success. See *House Ex. Doc.,* 39th Cong., 1st sess., vol. 1, pt. 3, ser. 1246, pp. 578-81.

64. Preston to Davis, June 28, 1864, Bigelow, *Retrospections,* II, 197.

65. Gwin to Montholon, October 15, 1865, Coleman, "Gwin's Plan," *Overland Monthly* 18 (August 1891): 209.

Bazaine. Despite Napoleon's instructions, the French general understood the feelings of Maximilian and the Mexicans. Thus, when Montholon took Gwin to military headquarters where he presented Napoleon's letter, Bazaine avoided Gwin, as he felt that the American's presence was too conspicuous at French headquarters.[66] Obviously disappointed by not seeing Bazaine at this time, Gwin settled for a secretly arranged meeting at Tacubaya, a suburb of Mexico City. Sara Yorke Stevenson, an observer of this initial Gwin-Bazaine interview, related the delicate planning necessary to introduce them casually at Casa Amarilla, the house rented by Colonel Talcott of Virginia, where Gwin was a guest.[67] After a long talk with Gwin, Bazaine left in good spirits. Aware that the Mexican ministry opposed the project, the general realized that a change in the imperial cabinet would be necessary before the plan could be implemented. Gwin, however, felt reassured by recurring talks with Bazaine, who told him that he would support the project despite Maximilian's opposition.[68]

Although Bazaine had advised Gwin not to call at the Palacio de México, the American disregarded this advice and received audiences on July 25 and 27, 1864, with Félix Éloin, Maximilian's Belgian chief of the cabinet.[69] Consistently antagonistic toward French-sponsored

---

66. Sara Yorke Stevenson, *Maximilian in Mexico: A Woman's Reminiscences of the French Intervention, 1862-1867* (New York: Century, 1899), p. 176; and McPherson, *William McKendree Gwin*, p. 256.

67. Stevenson, *Maximilian*, pp. 176-77. Claibourne stated that Montholon introduced Gwin to Bazaine; cited by Coleman, "Gwin's Plan," *Overland Monthly* 17 (May 1891): 498. Casa Amarilla in Tacubaya is presently an annex for the Archivo General de la Nación. Charles Griffin, ed., *Latin America: A Guide to the Historical Literature* (Austin: University of Texas Press, 1971), p. 377.

68. Stevenson, *Maximilian*, p. 177; and Gwin to his son, July 27, 1864, Coleman, "Gwin's Plan," *Overland Monthly* 18 (August 1891): 204.

69. Éloin was a mining engineer with close connections with the Belgian court. He had been pressed on Maximilian by Leopold I, father of Carlota. Leopold consistently advised Maximilian to defy French objectives in Sonora. See Baron Beyens, *Le Second Empire: Vu par un diplomate belge*, 2 vols. (Paris, Plon-Nourrit et cie, 1925), I, 266-67; Albert Duchesne, *L'expédition des volontaires belges au Mexique 1864-1867*, 2 vols. (Bruxelles, Musée Royal de l'armée et d'histoire militaire, 1967-68), I, 141-42; and Éloin to Hidalgo, October 29, 1865, Maximilian and Carlota Collection, Charlotte-Éloin Papers, box 1.

projects, Éloin intimated that Gwin should have applied for an interview with the emperor before talking to Bazaine. Gwin interestingly concluded that the Belgian had adopted the prejudices of the Mexicans against Americans. To Éloin, however, the former California politician represented the potential fulfillment of Napoleon's plan to obtain Sonora's silver, an irritation for Belgians, who resented French control of their own monetary policies. On the day following Gwin's meeting with Éloin, the French minister to Mexico, Montholon, reported to his foreign minister that Maximilian stubbornly refused to implement the Sonoran proposals.[70]

Gwin was palpably involved in a delicate mission. On the same evening of the July 27 Éloin meeting, he met again with Bazaine at Casa Amarilla. When Gwin relayed the results of his apparently fruitless interview with Éloin, Bazaine replied that Éloin was unreliable, but "could be bought."[71] Frustrated, but wiser, Gwin now relied on Bazaine for fulfillment of Napoleon's development of Sonora.

Gwin prematurely rejoiced that the general himself would lead the expedition to Sonora. Nevertheless, the extensive rumors that Americans, with Gwin as their leader, planned to detach this area from Mexico, troubled Gwin. Plainly uneasy about the Éloin interview, he told his son to convey a letter to Morny, hoping to insure that no instructions countermanding the expedition were issued. With resilient optimism, and revealing previous plans in Paris, Gwin also directed his son to encourage Morny to send both funds and men to implement the plans for Sonora.[72] However, Gwin had reason to fear impending adversity. Joaquín Velásquez de León, minister-president of the Mexican empire, wrote Gwin two weeks later that Maximilian was unable to receive him. Directing Gwin to another official, Velásquez de León curtly advised him to observe circumspection and brevity.[73]

---

70. Éloin to Gwin, July 23, 1864; Gwin to his son, July 27, 1864, Coleman, "Gwin's Plan," *Overland Monthly* 18 (August 1891): 204, 212; and Montholon to Drouyn de Lhuys, July 28, 1864, Ollivier, *La intervencion francesa,* p. 137.

71. Gwin to his son, July 27, 1864, Coleman, "Gwin's Plan," *Overland Monthly* 18 (August 1891): 204.

72. Ibid.; and Morny to Gwin, Jr., September 17, 1864, ibid., 205.

73. Velásquez de León to Gwin, August 12, 1864, ibid., 212.

During the same period that the Mexican court rejected Gwin, the French court applied more pressure on Maximilian. The three major French financial advisors on Mexican affairs—Germiny, Fould and Corta—alleged that the unresolved Sonoran issue hindered further economic support to Mexico.[74] French military forces continued plans to press northward. The United States minister to Mexico wrote Seward that two to four thousand French soldiers would be sent to Sonora in October to make the state into a French colony, in order to reimburse military expenses. Unsure of privileges granted to Gwin, Corwin observed that Maximilian and the Mexicans deplored the possibility of Sonora becoming more independent of the central government.[75]

Seward received this news about his old friend Gwin in a spirit of revival of a former rivalry. The secretary of state wryly commented to Dayton that Gwin would turn out to be "even more of an inconvenience to whatever government may exist in Mexico than of ultimate harm to our own country." Notwithstanding, he instructed his minister to France to ascertain Gwin's support from Napoleon.[76] The French emperor substantially backed Gwin. It had been only one year since the senator had arrived in Paris, conferred with two emperors, received encouragement that would enable him to recoup his financial fortunes, and had expectantly recrossed the Atlantic.

In September of 1864, referring to Napoleon's personal request for straightforward views of political and military affairs, Gwin lauded the French army's current successful campaign to take possession of Sinaloa and to advance towards Sonora and Chihuahua by October. Asking for continued military support, Gwin reinforced Napoleon's objective of obtaining Sonora's mineral wealth in exchange for Mexico's debts to France. The Mexican empire would also benefit from the development of Sonora; with renewed wealth and population, it would thus be enabled to defend itself against foreign or domestic enemies.[77]

---

74. Hidalgo to Maximilian, July 15, 1864, HHUSA, Max., box 19, pt. 2, pp. 333-34.
75. Thomas Corwin to Seward, August 29, 1864, NA, State, MD Mex., microcopy 97, roll 31, vol. 30.
76. Seward to Dayton, September 15, 1864, *Senate Ex. Doc.,* 38th Cong., 2nd sess., vol. 1, set 1209, doc. 11, p. 146.
77. Gwin to Napoleon III, September 12, 1864, Coleman, "Gwin's Plan," *Overland Monthly* 17 (May 1891): 506-08.

In this letter Gwin revealed none of his later animosity toward Bazaine, now a marshal, nor any difficulty in contacting him.[78] Bazaine had carefully examined the plan and had indicated it could be implemented when the French army entered Sonora. Although he discerningly suggested changing Gwin's projected system of land donation to one of preemption, as used in the United States, Gwin agreed with this revision and the idea that it would increase the public revenue. Throughout Gwin's letter to Napoleon, however, a wariness is unmistakable. Colonel Charles Blanchot, a member of Bazaine's staff, observed, "I saw this venerable American and was a witness of his restlessness, of his disillusions, and of his anger" at the obstinacy of Maximilian. Claiming that Bazaine earnestly tried to help, Blanchot realized that fulfillment of Gwin's plans depended on Maximilian's acceptance of the February 1864 treaty between Montholon and the Regency.[79]

Some two weeks after writing Napoleon, Gwin presented mining plans to the empress through Charles Corta, a member of the *corps législatif* and Maximilian's French financial advisor, who read them to Carlota. Gwin believed that the interview between Corta and Carlota was favorable although the empress, "being a woman," raised many objections. Carlota first exclaimed that Napoleon and Gwin wanted to take all of Mexico. But as she perused the document, she would say, "That is important, this is more important, and well, if France gets much, Mexico gets more." According to Gwin, Carlota agreed to everything except the duty-free exportation of bullion.[80] Displaying his first

---

78. Bazaine was promoted to Marshal of France on September 5, 1864. Dabbs, *The French Army in Mexico,* p. 116.

79. Gwin to Napoleon III, September 12, 1864, Coleman, "Gwin's Plan," *Overland Monthly* 17 (May 1891): 507. Thus the land laws of the United States and the Mexican mining code, adopted from the Spanish Ordinances of 1783, would be the legal provisions to develop the mineral resources of Sonora. Blanchot, *L'Intervention Française,* II, 257.

80. Gwin to his wife, September 29, 1864, Coleman, "Gwin's Plan," *Overland Monthly* 17 (May 1891): 508; and Gwin to his daughter, September 29, 1864, ibid., 508-09. But when the papers were actually presented to Carlota for her signature, in the emperor's absence, she refused to sign them, saying she dreaded to face Maximilian's anger if she did so. McPherson, *William McKendree Gwin,* p. 260. For the British reaction to the plan for duty-free export of silver, see foreign minister to Cowley, February 15, 1865, PRO/FO, 27/1555, no. 108.

dissatisfaction with Bazaine's support, Gwin philosophically accepted Carlota's modifications which, he felt, Montholon would also approve. With his spirits restored by the Carlota conference, Gwin looked forward to defending the treaty against Maximilian's objections, and he immediately began preparing a system of government for Sonora.[81]

Gwin's memorandum to accompany Montholon's treaty granting a concession of the mines of north Mexico to France was a major effort to convince Maximilian and Carlota of the need to develop the mineral and agricultural resources there. He urged for an immediate decision, as this area was held by Juárez, who might induce soldiers from the United States to join his cause by offering them mines. Thus, Napoleon's army must occupy northern Mexico since even the United States would "pause before firing a shot at the French flag." Noting that Mexico was in the same condition as it had been in 1821, Gwin pointed out the precedent policy of the independent government, which had reduced silver duties drastically, enabling foreign investors to restore damaged mines.[82]

Reminding the new rulers that the government's power, merely "a shadow" in Sonora, had hitherto failed to subdue either rebellious governors or relentless Indians, Gwin deplored the fact that the richest mines of the entire empire continued to be neglected.[83] Rich surface ores would need relatively little foreign capital and labor to produce great amounts of bullion. Strongly advocating laissez-faire policies, Gwin claimed that the settlement of Sonora would insure rapid development of its mineral and agricultural wealth, which he extravagantly insisted was unparalleled in the history of the world. Dismissing the idea of expected revenue from exported bullion, the point Carlota had insisted upon, he emphasized increased income from custom duties on imported goods and from internal taxation of immigrants. Since northern Mexico was on the route to

---

81. Gwin to his wife, September 29, 1864, Coleman, "Gwin's Plan," *Overland Monthly* 17 (May 1891): 508; and Gwin to his daughter, September 29, 1864, ibid., 508-09.

82. "Memorandum Accompanying the Project of a Treaty Giving a Concession of the Mines of North Mexico to France," ibid., 509-10. This is the memorandum read to Carlota by Corta in September 1864.

83. Ibid. Gwin had made similar statements while a senator. Gwin, "Memoirs," p. 275.

Europe from the East Indies, China, and Japan, both world trade and the developed mines would quickly restore public credit, guarantee the permanency of the empire, and eliminate all of its liabilities.[84]

Rumors began circulating immediately that negotiations had already been concluded for French control over both Sonora and Lower California. Gwin, portrayed as inducing intrigues among Northerners as well as Southerners, would supposedly develop Mexican mines that were either sold or mortgaged to the French for reimbursement of Mexico's debts to France.[85] Maximilian, also perceiving Gwin as a dangerous opportunist, refused to approve plans which would violate Mexican territory. Irritated, the French emperor remonstrated that Gwin was simply an entrepreneur: "It is obvious that these men of business hope to make money."[86]

Napoleon pointedly encouraged Maximilian to be more flexible in his relationship with Gwin:

> I venture to say that in labouring to found a new empire it is impossible to arrive at perfection all at once; the measures that one takes always offer certain advantages accompanied by certain disadvantages; the cleverness of the sovereign consists in seeing whether the former outweigh the latter.—The same is the case with regard to the question of Sonora. I know that Mr. Gwyn's projects have not met with favour in Mexico, and yet he is the man best able to be of service in that country.[87]

Using Gwin's arguments, Napoleon then sternly advised the Mexican emperor to take a more positive position on plans for Sonora:

> It is feared in Mexico that Sonora may become an American province, but, believe me, even if nothing is done, it will become

---

84. "Memorandum Accompanying the Project of a Treaty Giving a Concession of the Mines of North Mexico to France," Coleman, "Gwin's Plan," *Overland Monthly* 17 (May 1891): 510-12.

85. Romero to Seward, December 3, 1864, enclosing synopsis of a letter, dated November 22, 1864, from an unidentified friend of Romero's in New York. *House Ex. Doc.,* 39th Cong., 1st sess., vol. 1, pt. 3, set 1246, doc. 1, pp. 498-99.

86. Napoleon III to Maximilian, November 16, 1864, Corti, *Maximilian,* II, 853. By comparing this letter with Gwin's memorandum to the French emperor of September 1864, Gwin's influence is evident.

87. Ibid., 853-54.

one by force of circumstances. Colonists and adventurers are already entering the province one by one, and as soon as a great number of them are there, without government organization and control, they will declare themselves independent. This will not happen if the Government places itself at the head of the immigration, plants its flag there, and organizes the country.[88]

Clearly under financial stress, Maximilian appeared to relent. He assured Napoleon that the establishment in Sonora of a government "under the simultaneous protection of the French and Mexican flags is the object of all my care, and will, I hope, enable me in a not too distant future to enhance the resources of this interesting portion of my vast empire." The Mexican emperor's cynicism is apparent when he adds that he would then "be charmed to see Mr. Gwyn attract there the many American colonists who appear to be merely awaiting a sign from him to come and group themselves round him to seek their fortune."[89]

Maximilian was not "charmed" to see Gwin attract American colonists to Sonora; the support of the Mexican emperor continued to elude the senator.[90] Uneasy about American colonists, Maximilian may have been hopeful that the convention between Austria and Mexico would provide him with European colonists.[91] His antagonism towards Gwin appears to be especially evident in November 1864. As late as October, Gwin had been socially included in the

---

88. Ibid., 854.
89. Maxmilian to Napoleon III, December 27, 1864, ibid., 861-62.
90. According to Kathryn Abbey Hanna, "The Roles of the South in the French Intervention in Mexico," *Journal of Southern History* 20 (February 1954): 15, the French abandoned the idea of developing Sonora's mines as early as November 1864. However, the November and December correspondence between the two emperors in that year indicates animated interest.
91. This convention, ratified on April 14, 1865, provided Maximilian with military volunteers from Austria and contained specific provisions for Austrian emigration and colonization. *Reichs-Gesetz-Blatt für das Kaiserthum Oesterreich,* Wien, *Convention zwischen Oesterreich und Mexico,* October 19, 1864, articles 2, 4, 10; Rare Book Room, Fondren Library, Rice University. However, of the various sources of potential immigrants, only the Americans provided more than their brawn and misery. They brought families, capital, entrepreneurs, managers and a spirit of enterprise others lacked. Blondeel to Rogier, July 22, 1865, AEB,CP, Mex., vol. 1, no. 90.

marriage festivities for Montholon's daughter. At that time Gwin still expressed respect for Maximilian and Carlota, although he was obviously disappointed that, at these ceremonies, the emperor never alluded to his discussion with Gwin in Paris about Sonora. During the wedding breakfast the empress's chamberlain, Count Charles de Bombelles, indicated that the delay was not because of opposition to the plan for Sonora but rather "a pause" to determine if Gwin's project "would stand fire."[92] Also in October, continued enthusiasm was manifest when Gwin sat next to Marshal Bazaine at another function, where Sonora was the main topic of conversation.[93]

Before Maximilian's arrival in Mexico, the French had been able to resolve most of their difficulties with the Regency in favor of France. By November, however, the Mexican emperor had begun to assert his own authority. His new ministerial appointments, regarded by Bazaine as esteemed by Mexican liberals and a wise tactical move to obtain support for the empire, were all anti-French.[94] Another complicating factor was the political and military situation in the United States. Although Lincoln expected his administration to be repudiated in the November 1864 election, he was reelected by a large majority. Thus, the Lincoln policies would be continued, and in December the end of the Civil War seemed very near.[95]

By the end of 1864, the Mexican government exhibited an independence and nationalism that doomed the Sonoran plans of Napoleon and Gwin. Ironically, it is at this time that General Armand Alexandre Castagny finally entered Sonora, one of the last areas to hold out for Juárez.[96]

---

92. Gwin to his daughter, October 1864, Coleman, "Gwin's Plan," *Overland Monthly* 17 (May 1891): 514-15.
93. Gwin to his daughter, October 1864, ibid., 206-07.
94. Bazaine to the French minister of war, no. 53, November 27, 1864, Bazaine Archives, vol. 11, f. 2013-15; also in Genaro García, ed., *Colección de documentos inéditos o muy raros para la historia de México,* 30 vols. (México: Librería de la Vda. de Ch. Bouret, 1908-10), vol. XXIV, doc. 8, pp. 33-43; Bazaine to the French minister of war, no. 54, December 10, 1864, Bazaine Archives, vol. 11, f. 2047-49. José Fernando Ramírez, particularly hostile to France, became minister of foreign affairs. Desternes and Chandet, *Maximilien et Charlotte,* p. 234.
95. Bemis, *American Secretaries of State,* VII, 102-03.
96. Dabbs, *French Army in Mexico,* pp. 99, 241.

Gwin was not with Castagny and, cognizant that his efforts were being frustrated by Maximilian, he again turned to Napoleon. On January 19, 1865, he left Mexico for France, hoping that he could induce the French emperor to intercede for him more vigorously. Maximilian's self-reliance, already in evidence by late 1864, waxed during the first six months of 1865 and was to culminate in his total repudiation of the French emperor's plans for Sonora.

Chapter Seven

The End of French Efforts to Control Sonora

—————•—————

French attempts to attain a lien on Sonora's silver mines increased during the first six months of 1865. Having previously failed to obtain Maximilian's approval through diplomacy, Napoleon took advantage of military events in the United States to frighten the Mexican emperor into acquiescence. This, too, was to end in frustration.

Military threats from the United States in the first part of 1865, the end of the Civil War, surreptitious aid to Juárez, and the critical two-month loss of Seward's influence on American foreign policy alarmed Maximilian. By the latter part of June, however, encouraged by both Napoleon's assurances of continued support and by Seward's restored and restraining influence on military actions along the Rio Grande, the Mexican emperor continued to thwart French attempts to obtain Sonora's mines.

As French troops marched toward Sonora in late 1864, leaving without William McKendree Gwin, apprehension had spread about the success of Napoleon's plans. Hostile editorials and unfavorable reports about Gwin began appearing in January 1865.[1] *El pájaro verde,* the most conservative Mexican newspaper, protested that immigrants from the United States, if allowed to settle near the northern frontier, would be the ruin of Mexico. A disappointed and discouraged Gwin conferred with the French minister and then

---

1. Luis de Arroyo, Mexican consul in New York, to his minister of foreign affairs, January 3, and February 7, 1865, Lefévre, *Documents officiels,* II, 101-02.

decided to consult further with the Duc de Morny and the French emperor.[2]

On January 19, 1865, the same day that Gwin left for Paris, John Bigelow, United States minister to France after William L. Dayton's death the previous month, met with the French foreign minister. Bigelow frankly asked Drouyn de Lhuys to explain his perturbing remark that French relations with the United States were "friendly, though delicate—delicate." Leading the conversation to Sonora, Bigelow inquired about reports circulating in newspapers and at clubs that Maximilian had ceded, or was about to cede, Sonora to France. In this first—and last—candid French discussion of Sonora, Drouyn de Lhuys carefully responded that while no outright cession of territory was involved, negotiations were in process to obtain a lien on Sonora's mineral products in order to secure Mexican indebtedness to France.[3] Eleven days later José Manuel Hidalgo, Maximilian's minister to France, complained to his sovereign that the rumored cession of Sonora had stirred up much controversy. Stunned about the possibility of further dismemberment of Mexico and stating that "Sonora *must* be for us," Hidalgo emphatically denied the cession. Admitting that the formation of Franco-Mexican mining companies to develop Sonora's mines would be profitable and acceptable, Hidalgo was confused about talk of complete cession, a topic neither Maximilian nor Drouyn de Lhuys had ever mentioned to him. The Mexican minister was irritated by both Montholon's protection of Gwin and by the possibility of colonists from the United States settling in Sonora. Sympathetic with Napoleon's expectation that

---

2. Alfred J. Hanna and Kathryn Abbey Hanna, "The Immigration Movement of the Intervention and Empire as Seen Through the Mexican Press," *Hispanic American Historical Review* 27 (May 1947): 233, citing *El párajo verde,* February 14, 1865. Generally amenable to Confederate emigrants if they were not permitted close to Mexico's borders, *El párajo verde* balked at extension of religious toleration for foreigners. Ibid., pp. 224, 230; and McPherson, *William McKendree Gwin,* p. 261.

3. Bigelow to Seward, January 20, 1865, *House Ex. Doc.,* 39th Cong., 1st sess., vol. 1, pt. 3, ser. 1246, doc. 1, pp. 361-62. This backing away from the cession of Sonora is consistent with Drouyn de Lhuys' correspondence with Montholon. See Monthlon to Drouyn de Lhuys, January 8, 1865 and Drouyn de Lhuys to Montholon, January 14, 1865, AEF, CP, Mex., vol. 63.

Mexican silver be sent to France and not to England, Hidalgo insisted that total cession was neither necessary nor advisable to satisfy
French requests. Extremely uncomfortable, Hidalgo underscored his
statement, *"I do not even want to admit the discussion about this."*[4]

Discussion, however, increased. Before Seward received Bigelow's
January report of France's admitted interest in Sonora's mines, star-
tling events were taking place in the United States. The Hampton
Roads conference, proposing a joint expedition into Mexico by both
Northern and Southern military leaders in alliance with Juárez, was
offered as a method for ending the Civil War by uniting both factions
against common enemies: the French and the Mexican Imperialists.
Conceived in December 1864 by the journalist Francis Preston Blair,
the plan appeared authentically ominous; Blair's two sons were
Montgomery Blair, a member of President Lincoln's cabinet, and
Francis P. Blair, Jr., a general in the Union army. Receiving permis-
sion from Lincoln to pass through army lines, Blair arrived in
Richmond where he presented the proposal to the president of the
Confederacy on January 12, 1865. Although Jefferson Davis, like
Lincoln, was cautious about direct commitments, he presumably
agreed. Events then moved swiftly. Three weeks later, on February 3,
President Lincoln and Secretary of State Seward met with
Confederate delegates on the *River Queen* at Hampton Roads. After
a four-hour conference, the project crumbled over whether an
armistice or surrender should be concluded before beginning the
joint invasion of Mexico.[5]

Although later analysis suggested that the Hampton Roads conference was not taken seriously by any of the Civil War leaders,[6] the
mere possibility of such a plan stunned both Napoleon and

---

4. Hidalgo to Maximilian, January 30, 1865, HHUSA, Max., karton 19, pt. 3,
   docs. 657-63. For Bazaine's harrassment and diversion to France of bullion
   initially earmarked for Britain, see minister of foreign affairs to Cowley,
   February 18, 1865 and admiralty to Cowley, February 1, 1865, PRO/FO,
   27/1555, nos. 61, 64, 68 and 82. Also foreign office to Cowley, March 9,
   1865, ibid., 27/1556, no. 193.
5. Case and Spencer, *Civil War Diplomacy,* pp. 560-66; and Hanna and
   Hanna, *Napoleon III and Mexico,* pp. 209-14.
6. Elizabeth Brett White, *American Opinion of France: From Lafayette to
   Poincaré* (New York: Alfred A. Knopf, 1927), p. 165.

Maximilian. Information about Blair's proposal may have reached Napoleon as early as February 3, the day of the conference, for on that date Eugénie wrote Carlota, "The Emperor has just told me that for the moment there will be no reduction in the army."[7] Since rumors about Sonora had circulated throughout 1864, possibly they had some influence on the conception of Blair's plan. Thomas Corwin, United States minister to Mexico, later stated, "with positive certainty," that Maximilian had acceded to the French demands in late 1864 or early 1865.[8] However, on December 28, 1864, Maximilian had obstinately referred to the development of Sonora as proceeding "under the simultaneous protection of the French and Mexican flags."[9] The Blair project was a timely device for the French emperor to use in persuading Maximilian.

The French chargé in Washington, Louis de Geoffroy, reported two detailed accounts of the pending conference ten days before it took place.[10] The Quai d'Orsay received this alarming correspondence on February 6. Interestingly, the French officially denied the cession of Sonora in *Le Moniteur Universel* two days later.[11] A week after learning of the proposed conference, however, for the first time during the Civil War, the French minister of finance intimated that the United States and France might go to war—over Mexico.[12] Talk and intrigues about Sonora increased. Hidalgo learned that the mining engineer, Félix Éloin, Maximilian's Belgian advisor, accompanied by agents, was going to Sonora in disguise on a secret mission. Éloin had reluctantly concluded that some guarantees to the French about Sonoran resources was the most practical way to assure French troops remaining in

7. Eugénie to Carlota, February 3, 1865 and Napoleon to Maximilian, March 1, 1865, Corti, *Maximilian,* II, 887-89; Comte Emile de Kératry, *L'Empereur Maximilien: Son élévation et sa chute* (Amsterdam: L. Van Bakkenes, 1867), pp. 75-76.

8. Corwin to Seward, July 22, 1865, NA, State, MD Mex., vol. 30, microcopy 97, roll 32.

9. Maximilian to Napoleon, December 27, 1865, Corti, *Maximilian,* II, 860-62.

10. Case and Spencer, *Civil War Diplomacy,* pp. 560-61, citing Geoffroy to Drouyn de Lhuys, January 24, 1865.

11. *Le Moniteur Universel,* February 8, 1865.

12. Case and Spencer, *Civil War Diplomacy,* p. 563, citing Bigelow to Seward, February 14, 1865.

Mexico. By the end of February there were even regrets about the position Maximilian had taken about a cession of Sonora and in particular about Gwin's departure. Éloin's mission, its objectives unstated, may have concerned cession of Sonora's mines, but Hidalgo is most emphatic that Sonora itself had not been ceded. Citing the "absurd" news that not only Sonora but also Chihuahua, Sinaloa, Baja California, and Durango had been ceded to France, the whole to be administered by Gwin as Napoleon's viceroy, Hidalgo planned to issue a public denial in *Le Moniteur Universel* with Drouyn de Lhuys's approval.13 If Hidalgo is to be believed, admittedly a precarious assumption, he apparently knew nothing of Napoleon's plans. A month later Napoleon proposed the expansion of French control over this same region of northern Mexico, with the exception of Baja California.

Meanwhile, even before the results of the Union-Confederate talks were known in Paris, additional French troops were being prepared on short notice for shipment to Mexico.14 Geoffroy's dispatch containing the results of the Hampton Roads conference was received in Paris on February 21. Accurately reporting the actual conversations exchanged on the *River Queen,* Geoffroy acknowledged that the conference had failed; however, some of his interpretations were misleading and created genuine fear of a coalition against Mexico and France.15 In Paris Drouyn de Lhuys discounted reports that the United States was about to invade Mexico but indicated that if such an aggression were attempted, it would be forcibly opposed by France. Meanwhile, French troops in Mexico were "massed for action" and Bazaine confidently expected that at the first hostile move by the United States, he would "immediately" be sent an army of 100,000 to command.16 The ensuing tension between the United States and France was the most critical of the entire Civil War.

---

13. Hidalgo to Maximilian, February 14, 1865, HHUSA, Max., karton 19, pt. 3, docs. 690-91. Montholon to Drouyn de Lhuys, January 8 and February 27, 1865, AEF, CP, Mex., vol. 63.

14. Bigelow to Seward, February 17, 1865, *House Ex. Doc.,* 39th Cong., 1st sess., vol. 1, pt. 3., ser. 1246, doc. 1, p. 366.

15. Case and Spencer, *Civil War Diplomacy,* p. 560, citing Geoffroy to Drouyn de Lhuys, February 7, 1865.

16. Foreign minister to Cowley, May 4, 1865, PRO/FO, 27/1558, no. 384; and Blondeel to Rogier, June 10, 1865, AEB, CP, Mex., vol. 1, no. 90.

While the Hampton Roads conference gravely alarmed the French and Mexican courts, it revived hope among Mexican Republicans. Matías Romero, Juárez's indefatigable minister to the United States, had approvingly heard of Blair's plan on January 10, 1865.[17] After learning of the proposal's failure, however, Romero tried to arouse Seward's animosity against France by reporting detailed rumors of the cession of Sonora. Romero dismissed Maximilian's hostility to such a cession on the basis that the Mexican emperor would not prevail against the wishes of Napoleon. Romero's letter bristled with bitter disappointment over the Hampton Roads talks, and Seward perfunctorily replied that the letter would be placed in the archives as evidence of Romero's patriotism.[18]

After receiving Bigelow's report of his conversation with Drouyn de Lhuys on January 19, Seward officially protested either a cession of, or a lien on, Sonora's mineral resources. However, the tone of his dispatch, written three days after he himself had talked with Confederate leaders about concerted military action against Mexico, was decidedly conciliatory. Referring to the Hampton Roads conference, Seward urged Bigelow to assure French leaders that there was no danger of action against either France or Mexico.[19] Nevertheless, reports continued to circulate that American military reserves from Arizona and Colorado territories were preparing to invade Sonora to thwart its cession to France and that Napoleon had appointed Gwin as viceroy.[20] Meanwhile, Montholon had received significant funds and hoped finally to close out the Jecker affair.[21]

While Franco-American relations were deteriorating, Gwin was

17. Hanna and Hanna, *Napoleon III and Mexico,* p. 210, citing Romero to Lerdo de Tejada, January 10, 1865.
18. Romero to Seward, February 6, 1865, and Seward to Romero, February 25, 1865, *House Ex. Doc.,* 39th Cong., 1st sess., vol 1, pt. 3, ser. 1246, doc. 1, pp. 500-02.
19. Seward to Bigelow, February 7, 1865, ibid., p. 363.
20. Manuel Guillin, Mexican vice-consul in San Francisco, to his minister of foreign affairs, March 9, 1865, HHUSA, Max., karton 141, docs. 3-4.
21. Montholon to Drouyn de Lhuys, January 28, 1865, AEF, CP, Mex., vol. 63. When Montholon left Mexico City on April 20, he had almost completed arrangements settling the Jecker affair. Montholon to Drouyn de Lhuys, March 25 and April 11, 1865, ibid.

en route to Paris where he arrived early in March 1865. There he was encouraged when the Duc de Morny, now seriously ill, sent word of his continued interest in Sonora. Morny promised Gwin a conference at the earliest possible moment; but as he died only four days later, it never materialized.[22] Well known for his encouragement of French investments in Mexico, Morny's death was unsettling to financiers and investors who had depended on his political influence. However, a measure of reassurance for them came on February 14 when the Council of Ministers authorized Bazaine to take over the finances of Mexico and force the payments allegedly due to France.[23]

However, there now emerged a force more cogent than Morny's prestige. Napoleon had decided to expand French predominance to Sinaloa, Durango, and Chihuahua, in addition to Sonora, and had requested Gwin to prepare a plan for its undertaking.[24] This enlargement, in view of Maximilian's earlier reluctance, can be explained by the threat of the Hampton Roads conference, the approaching end to the Civil War, the French army's recent invasions of northern Mexico, and nervousness in French financial circles.

Gwin, having previously been denied admission to Sonora, was understandably reserved about this new venture. He told the French emperor that he was willing to return if assured of French military support. Echoing Napoleon's earlier predilections, Gwin reiterated that revenues from customs duties and mines would be applied to the interest and, if sufficient, to the principal of the debt Mexico owed France. Then Napoleon could feel financially secure in making loans to Mexico. Assuming that Maximilian's major objection had been fear of losing northern Mexico to an influx of adventurers, Gwin emphasized that immigrants must be required to take an oath of allegiance to the Mexican Imperial government and that precautions

---

22. McPherson, *William McKendree Gwin,* p. 261, citing Éloin, to Gwin, March 6, 1865.
23. *La France* (Réone financière), March 13, 1865, and *Mémorial Diplomatique,* March 13, 1865, extracts in *House Ex. Doc.,* 39th Cong., 1st sess., vol. 1, pt. 3, ser. 1246, doc. 1, pp. 384-85. Fould to minister of war, February 14, 1865, AEF, CP, Mex., vol. 63.
24. Gwin to Napoleon, March 25, 1865, Coleman, "Gwin's Plan," *Overland Monthly,* 2nd ser., 17 (May 1891): 515-16.

should be taken to banish all enemies of the empire.[25] Exhibiting some of his old resiliency, Gwin prepared his last "memorandum" for the French emperor. Along with plans for the subjugation of both Indian tribes and Juáristas in Sonora, he pragmatically suggested that a concerted effort be made to carry out these new proposals during the rainy season, starting in June, to enable crops to be planted. Still confident that colonization of Sonora, with its "richest mines in Mexico," would allow withdrawal of the French army, Gwin foresaw eventual French military aid as consisting of a small number of troops to guard posts on the northern border. Without colonization he predicted that the French would probably either be forced to withdraw from Sonora or to maintain a large, expensive military force. Asserting that Bazaine had agreed with this assessment, Gwin insisted that Confederate emigrants would help support the empire and make it unassailable from the United States.[26]

With Gwin again in Paris, rumors increased. Rufus King at the United States legation in Rome asked the French ambassador, the Count de Sartiges, about the current talk in Europe that Maximilian had ceded certain provinces to Napoleon as security for material and financial aid. King had been informed that Gwin was forming a Confederate colony and would be viceroy of Sonora. Adhering to the official statement in *Le Moniteur Universel* on February 8, the count denied it.[27] At the very time that Gwin and Napoleon were preparing expansive plans for northern Mexico, Drouyn de Lhuys had heatedly protested United States newspaper stories about Gwin and French interests in Sonora. Instructed by Seward to calm French fears, Bigelow replied that in the United States "everybody's most idle thought and casual impression" might appear in the press although such articles did not necessarily reflect government opinion.[28] Yet

25. Ibid., p. 516.
26. "Memorandum for Emperor Napoleon from William McKendree Gwin," March 1865, ibid., pp. 516-19. See also Montholon to Drouyn de Lhuys, Jan. 8, 1865 AEF, CP, Mex., vol. 63.
27. King to Seward, Rome, March 4, 1865, *House Ex. Doc.,* 39th Cong. 1st sess., vol. 1, pt. 3, ser. 1246, doc. 1, p. 153.
28. Bigelow to Seward, March 17, 1865,State, *Diplomatic Correspondence,* 39th Cong., 1st sess., pt. 2, 1865, pp. 246-47.

over a month earlier, on February 9, 1865, Bigelow confided to his diary that Napoleon III stated he would like nothing better than to be out of Sonora altogether.[29]

The French then began a counterattack by claiming that three times since their presence in Mexico Juárez had offered to sell Sonora to the United States. With an oblique reference to the Hampton Roads conference, Charles Corta, the French financial advisor to Maximilian, asserted that Juárez's most recent offer had been directly to President Lincoln.[30] Although Gwin was still uneasy about obtaining Maximilian's approval, Juárez predicted that Maximilian would obediently obey Napoleon's demands to cede Sonora to France.[31] In March 1865, Juárez apprehensively watched events from an unenviable position. While Gwin and Napoleon discussed plans for northern Mexico, French troops—"the successors of Raousset, . . . those who covet our territorial riches,"—subdued Guaymas and spread throughout Sonora.[32]

In his last audience with the French emperor, Gwin received a letter commending him to Marshal Bazaine. In it Napoleon stated, "The Emperor hopes that the Emperor Maximilian will favor your projects, and the Marshal is ordered to support them near him,"[33] presumably meaning to support Maximilian's French financial advisors. The Juárist colonel Enrique A. Mejía was inexplicably shown the original of this letter, which he interpreted as an attempt to form a barrier against the United States with Confederates who would create a hostile power on the border.[34]

---

29. Bigelow Papers, Diaries, February 9, 1865, pp. 49-51.
30. Speech of Charles Corta in the *corps législatif,* April 10, 1865, *Le Moniteur Universel,* April 11, 1865. This assertion was reported in the London *Times* and reproduced in the New York *World.* See the first enclosure in Dano to Drouyn de Lhuys, June 29, 1865, AEF, CP, Mex., vol. 63.
31. Lerdo de Tejada, foreign minister of the Mexican Republic, National Palace at Chihuahua, to Romero March 23, 1865, *House Ex. Doc.,* 39th Cong., 1st sess., vol. 1, pt. 3, ser. 1246, doc. 1, pp. 602-03.
32. "Proclamation of Ignacio Pesquiera," governor and military commander of Sonora, Camp at Santa María, March 30, 1865, ibid., p. 657.
33. Eugène Conti, secretary of the emperor and chief of the cabinet, to Gwin, March 31, 1865, Coleman, "Gwin's Plan," *Overland Monthly* 17 (June 1891): 595.
34. Mejía to Romero, July 1, 1865, *House Ex. Doc.,* 39th Cong., 1st sess., vol. 1, pt. 3, ser. 1246, doc., 1 p. 512.

Leaving Paris on April 1, 1865, Gwin arrived in Mexico City in early May, finding the Imperial government upset over the end of the Civil War, President Lincoln's assassination, and Secretary of State Seward's injuries. Maximilian, away in one of his periodic assessments of various states, and Bazaine, preoccupied with his own wedding plans, were still unavailable, unwilling, or unable to help him.[35] Animosity between Maximilian and Bazaine was now clearly evident in matters pertaining to Sonora. The Mexican press began criticizing the rumored cession of Mexican territory in April and May of 1865. In a move against French control, Maximilian released a number of editors who had been imprisoned for opposition to the military court and decreed freedom of the press on April 10.[36] Editorial comment against cession of Sonora or its mineral rights increased in nationalistic indignation, even though Bazaine fought back by fining and imprisoning several editors for joining in the outcry against alienation of Mexican territory.[37] Within Maximilian's Council of State were two factions, one favoring French interests and one opposed. In the latter camp the most obstinant, the liberal Jose Fernando Ramirez, was now foreign minister.[38] Clinging to hope of a rapprochement with the United States, and increasingly defying French policies, Maximilian was encouraged when Corwin praised the Mexican emperor's liberal programs.[39] His Belgian advisor promoted this optimism. Éloin, opposing both concessions to the French and Gwin's influx of Confederates in Sonora, assured Maximilian that the United States would not declare war on Mexico.[40] On the death of Lincoln Éloin suddenly left Mexico for Washington. He then proceeded to Paris and Brussels to report the

35. Gwin to his wife, May 11, 1865, Coleman, "Gwin's Plan," *Overland Monthly* 17 (June 1891): 593.
36. Hanna and Hanna, "The Immigration Movement," p. 224, citing *Diario del Imperio.*
37. Bancroft, *History of Mexico*, VI, 174.
38. Montholon to Drouyn de Lhuys, March 25 and April 11, 1865, AEF, CP, Mex., vol. 63.
39. Corwin to Ramírez, April 28, 1865, HHUSA, Max., karton 21, konvolut G, Dipl. Agenten in Nordamerika, pt. 3, docs. 43-45.
40. "Eloin Articulo," n.d., ibid., docs. 95-102; 1865 letters from Éloin, to Maximilian, ibid., karton 15, fasc. 8, konvolut 4.

"real truth" about Mexican affairs.[41] It was into this ambivalent atmosphere that Gwin, his confidence somewhat shaken, returned to Mexico.

Impatient with delays—"To think of our being kept here holding our hands, when those prodigious mines are inviting us to fortune"[42] —Gwin lost a major advocate when Montholon, reassigned as French ambassador to the United States, left Mexico for his new post only a few hours before his own arrival.[43] Gwin was regarded as France's unofficial agent, a dubious attribute at this time, and Bazaine supposedly assured Gwin that he would support his claims "to the utmost."[44] The earlier hostility of Maximilian's minister, Juan N. Almonte, presumably had been assuaged; in mid-May Almonte allegedly told Gwin that he had strong support.[45] Rumors of a further ministerial change, expected to take place the latter part of May, spread quickly because of the sudden removal of Éloin, hostile to French interests, from his position as Maximilian's advisor.[46]

Optimism balanced despair. The Jecker claims to one-third of Sonora's public lands presented another problem. Captain Charles P. Stone, the affiliate of Jecker's survey company a decade earlier, had taken the same steamer as Gwin from Havana to Mexico. Some of the Jecker claims had been settled on April 10, and Stone came to claim his own interests and to participate, independent of Gwin, in a project "of infinite importance" in the development of Sonora. Gwin was distressed to learn that a portion of Jecker's claims in Sonora were still

41. Dano to Drouyn de Lhuys, May 13 and June 11, 1865, AEF, CP, Mex., vol. 63.
42. Gwin, Jr., to his mother, May 16, 1865, *House Ex. Doc.,* 39th Cong., 1st sess., vol. 1, pt. 3, ser. 1246, doc. 1, p. 513.
43. Gwin to Montholon, October 15, 1865, Fort Jackson, Coleman, "Gwin's Plan," *Overland Monthly* 18 (August 1891): 209.
44. Stevenson, *Maximilian in Mexico,* p. 178.
45. Gwin, Jr., to his mother, May 16, 1865, *House Ex. Doc.,* 39th Cong., 1st sess., vol. 1, pt. 3, ser. 1246, doc. 1, p. 513. Almonte was perhaps reconciled to Gwin by the efforts of Thomas Massey, a close friend of both Almonte and Gwin. Comision secreta del Sr. Massey, Massey to Almonte, August 29, 1865; and Almonte to Massey, December 20, 1865, March 4 and 18, 1866, HHUSA, Max., karton 137, docs. 35-36, 39-41.
46. Gwin to his wife and daughters, May 16, 1865, *House Ex. Doc.,* 39th Cong., 1st sess., vol. 1, pt. 3, ser. 1246, doc. 1, pp. 513-14; and Massey to editor of New York *Daily News,* May 19, 1865, ibid., p. 515.

pending.[47] After Montholon's transfer, his successor, Alphonse Dano, had diligently worked on these as well as trying to settle all the initial claims which had helped lead to the intervention. However, he ran into a host of roadblocks, largely thrown up by Ramirez.[48] Bazaine urged Gwin to see Jecker directly and thus avoid any future difficulty about land for proposed colonists. Suggesting that he accumulate information about the authenticity of Jecker's claims and admonishing him not to attract attention by indiscreet inquiries, the French marshal then directed Gwin to consult Stone.[49] Although Gwin and Stone were in daily contact, Gwin resisted the suggestion to make an arrangement with Jecker. However, on the advice of another former U.S. senator, Louisiana's Pierre Soulé, who had talked to the Swiss banker, he changed his mind. According to Gwin, the result of meeting Jecker was that Gwin almost became the owner of Jecker's claim. Such an agreement, however, was never consummated.[50]

Maximilian was the ultimate, and most obstinate, obstacle to French plans for northern Mexico. Although he had been away from the capital since Gwin's return to Mexico in May, it was commonly believed that Napoleon would achieve his goals.[51] However, when the Mexican emperor returned to Mexico City, it was clear that neither personnel changes, military threats from the United States, nor French pressure had dampened his determination to maintain the integrity of

---

47. Blumberg, *Diplomacy of the Mexican Empire,* p. 72; Massey to editor of New York *Daily News,* May 19, 1865, *House Ex. Doc.,* 39th Cong., 1st sess., vol. 1, pt. 3, ser. 1246, doc. 1, pp. 515-16; and Gwin to his wife, n.d., but latter part of May 1865, Coleman, "Gwin's Plan," *Overland Monthly* 18 (August 1891): 208. Regarding procedures for Mexican indemnification of French subjects, see articles 14-16 in the Franco-Mexican convention negotiated at Miramar, April 10, 1864, reprinted in enclosure of Dayton to Seward, April 18, 1864, *Senate Ex. Doc.,* 38th Cong., 2nd sess., pt. 3, ser. 1209, doc. 452, pp. 74-75.
48. See especially Dano to Drouyn de Lhuys, June 28, 1865, AEF, CP, Mex., vol. 63. This is a detailed 28 page letter with 68 annexes.
49. Ludovic M. François de Noue, Bazaine's secretary, to Gwin, May 16, 1865, ibid.
50. Massey to Wood, May 18, 1865, *House Ex. Doc.,* 39th Cong., 1st sess., vol. 1, pt. 3, ser. 1246, doc. 1, p. 515; and Gwin to his wife, n.d., circa late May 1865, Coleman, "Gwin's Plan," *Overland Monthly* 18 (August 1891): 208.
51. Correspondence of the New Orleans *Times,* Vera Cruz, June 1, 1865, *House Ex. Doc.,* 39th Cong., 1st sess., vol. 1, pt. 3, ser. 1246, doc. 1, p. 517.

Mexican land. Maximilian had moreover fulfilled Napoleon's insistence on Mexican remuneration for French forces—without having to cede Sonora's mineral rights. Great quantities of Mexican silver had been sent to France, enabling the French monetary problem to stabilize for the first time since American and Australian gold had upset the bimetallic standard in 1851.[52] By June 1865, Chaix d'Est-Angé, vice-president of the French Council of State, admitted that Maximilian had carried out the Treaty of Miramar "with perfect exactness." He had reduced the Mexican debt to France, for all operations, from 39,458,000 francs to a negligible 500,000 to 600,000 francs. Mexican mining had been resumed with "extraordinary" results, while the customs duties at Tampico had quadrupled and those at Vera Cruz had doubled since Maximilian's arrival in Mexico.[53] The date of Chaix d'Est-Angé's speech, June 8, 1865, is significant. Less than twenty days later, on June 26, Maximilian publicly denied that Sonora had been ceded to France or that he had made any concessions to Napoleon's emissary, William McKendree Gwin.

Maximilian also had reason to feel more confident because of the French emperor's military firmness after the Hampton Roads conference. Shortly after the French learned of the actual discussion between Seward and Confederate leaders, Napoleon assured Maximilian that the United States would "think twice before declaring war" and that no more French troops would be recalled from Mexico.[54] Although Maximilian's fear of American intervention after the Civil War ended may have been behind his rejection of Napoleon's demands for Sonora, as the United States minister believed, French resistance to United States aid for Juárez flared anew in May of 1865.[55] European diplomats excitedly discussed French reaction to reports that disbanded officers

---

52. "Values of the Imports of Merchandise and Bullion into England, France, and the United States, from Mexico, 1857-1871," *Hansard's: Currency*, appendix, p. 708; and *Enquête sur les principes et les faits généraux qui régissent la circulation monétaire et fiduciaire*, VI, 534-35.

53. Discussion in the *corps législatif*, Thursday, June 8, 1865, *Le Moniteur Universel*, June 9, 1865. This admission had also been made by Eugène Rouher, secretary of state, on April 10, 1865, *Le Moniteur Universel*, April 11, 1865.

54. Napoleon to Maximilian, March 1, 1865, Corti, *Maximilian*, II, 887-88.

55. Corwin to Seward, July 22, 1865, NA, State, MD Mex., vol. 30, microcopy 97, roll 32.

and men of the Union army were joining the Juáristas.[56] General Ulysses S. Grant, who looked on Juárez as the Lafayette or Garibaldi of Mexico, appeared particularly threatening during the absence of Seward's restraining influence.[57] The French decisively supported Maximilian, and by the latter part of May 1865 Bigelow feared that Napoleon's hostility against aid to Juárez would explode into a war with the United States.[58]

As war possibilities increased, Maximilian's minister to the United States wrote that Californians, in support of both the Monroe Doctrine and the Juaristas, were preparing to invade Sonora. However, according to his sources close to Seward, he reported that the United States would not intervene if assured that Mexico's northern frontier would not be ceded to France.[59] This word of hope undoubtedly had great influence on Maximilian. He could avoid United States intervention and maintain Mexican territory, but only at the price of alienating France. Throughout May and early June, the threat of war increased. Alarmed by military actions of Generals Ulysses Grant and Philip Sheridan toward Mexico, Seward feared actual confrontation of American and French troops. A further complication were 14,000 Confederate troops in Texas, commanded by General Slaughter, who wished to enter Mexico as subjects of Maximilian. By the end of June, 1865 the French minister reported that Confederates were then pouring into Mexico.[60]

Resuming his duties in June after a two-month disability, Seward assured Napoleon that the United States would continue to observe

56. King to Seward, May 24, 1865, *House Ex. Doc.,* 39th Cong., 1st sess., vol. 1, pt. 2, ser. 1246, doc. 1, p. 159.

57. Mariano Degollado to Castillo, Mexican minister of foreign affairs, HHUSA, Max., karton 141, doc. 555.

58. Seward to Bigelow, June 12, 1865, restating Bigelow's dispatch of late May 1865, *House Ex. Doc.,* 39th Cong., 1st sess., vol. 1, pt. 3, ser. 1246, doc. 1, p. 393.

59. Luis de Arroyo to Castillo, May 22, 1865, HHUSA, Max., karton 141, docs. 41-43.

60. Bemis, *American Secretaries of State,* VII, 108. Blondeel to Rogier, May 27, 1865, AEB, CP, Mex., vol. 1, no. 86; and Dano to Drouyn de Lhuys, June 29, 1865, AEF, CP, Mex., vol. 63. The best study of the Confederate influx is Andrew F. Rolle, *The Lost Cause: The Confederate Exodus to Mexico,* (Norman, University of Oklahoma, 1965.)

neutrality. In his first letter since the April assassination attempt, Seward disavowed the "hasty language" of American newspapers and tried to calm escalating tensions between the two countries. Informing Bigelow of steps taken to prevent illicit armaments reaching Juárez, Seward earnestly hoped that if unavoidable incidents should occur, in spite of government restraints, these would be overlooked by France in order to maintain peace between the two countries.[61] Such incidents, as Seward had predicted, did indeed occur.[62] Throughout June of 1865 the United States pursued a conciliatory policy, and reports began to reach Maximilian that the American people wanted peace and order in Mexico as well as the opportunity to invest in Mexican mining ventures.[63]

Seward's efforts for peace were timely. Contrary to earlier reports from Bigelow and Romero that the *corps législatif* was hostile to French military expenditures in Mexico, the debates of June 9 ended in a vote of 232 to a mere 13, in favor of maintaining French troops there.[64] Napoleon asked his minister of the navy for a report on the possibility of transporting 100,000 more troops to Mexico and on engaging in naval warfare, without British support, against the United States.[65]

Maximilian was relieved that French troops would remain, and might even be augmented. It was perhaps because of this assurance that he became increasingly assertive about his own control of Mexican affairs. Certainly after the spring of 1865 Maximilian was neither the

---

61. Drouyn de Lhuys to Montholon, July 6, 1865, referring to a letter from Seward to Bigelow, received by Bigelow June 29, 1865, *House Ex. Doc.,* 39th Cong., 1st sess., vol. 1, pt. 3, ser. 1246, doc. 1, p. 693. See also Drouyn de Lhuys to Cowley, June 29, 1865, PRO/FO, 519/207, part III, no. 1177.

62. Correspondence between General E. B. Brown and General Tomás Mejía, about confrontations on the Rio Grande, HHUSA, Max., karton 24, fasc. 13, no. 16.

63. Memoir to Maximilian from E. de Courcillon, June 28, 1865, Correspondenzen aus den Vereinigten Staaten, ibid., karton 137, docs. 75-78.

64. *Le Moniteur Universel,* June 10, 1865. *Le Moniteur Universel,* June 9, 1865 set the number of French troops in Mexico in 1865 at approximately 22,000; Napoleon stated that the figure was 30,940. Napoleon to Maximilian, April 12, 1866, Corti, *Maximilian,* II, 933.

65. Captain Hore, British naval attaché in Paris, to Earl Russell, June 30, 1865, reporting a conversation with Admiral Page, president of the "Conseil des travaux de la Marine." The date of the conversation is not stated, although Hore noted it took place "some short time ago." Extracts in Case and Spencer, *Civil War Diplomacy,* p. 563.

"pawn" nor the "puppet" of France that historical tradition has made him.[66] His independence is particularly revealed in his denial of Sonora to France. Mexican nationalism, to Bazaine's distress, grew stronger—with the Mexican emperor's encouragement.[67] After Maximilian established freedom of the press, in defiance of the French marshal, in April of 1865, Mexican newspapers assumed a more nationalistic, anti-French posture. *El pájaro verde* reproduced a New York *Express* article, critically asserting that Gwin, accompanied by French troops, was actually en route to Sonora.[68] Public antagonism against French interests in Sonora were growing more articulate each day.

Finally, on June 26, 1865, Maximilian publicly denied the cession of Sonora's mines to France. The official newspaper of the Mexican Empire, *El Diario del Imperio,* stating that the emperor would be faithful to his oath and would "maintain and defend the integrity of the national territory with inflexible energy of will," disavowed any government connection with Napoleon's entrepreneur, William McKendree Gwin. The front-page newspaper article denounced projected plans to apply the entire production of Sonora to the debts owed the French government. Citing reports from American newspapers on the alleged cession of Sonora, *El Diario del Imperio* contemptuously stated, "Dr. Gwin figures in all of these stories, now as Governor, again as Viceroy and with the title of Duke, attributing power and authority derived from the Emperor of Mexico and France."[69]

Realizing that the bitter attack was a direct confrontation with Napoleon, the French minister to Mexico was stunned and expected a retraction.[70] Although Montholon admitted that the proposed cession of Sonora's mines was the major source of strained diplomatic relations

---

66. Dabbs, *The French Army in Mexico,* p. 134.
67. Even the covers of imperial sheet music underwent change. In 1864 both the Austrian and Mexican insignias are displayed, side by side, but by 1865 only the Mexican insignia is used. Music Sheets Z 33174 RBR, Maximilian and Carlota Collection, Fondren Library, Rice University, Houston, Texas.
68. McPherson, *William McKendree Gwin,* p. 266. Dano to Drouyn de Lhuys, June 11, 1865, AEF, CP, Mex., vol. 63.
69. *El Diario del Imperio,* June 26, 1865, enclosed in a dispatch from Corwin to Seward, July 11, 1865, NA, State, MD Mex., vol. 30, microcopy 97, roll 31.
70. Dano to Drouyn de Lhuys, June 29, 1865, Díaz, *Versión francesa,* IV, 135-38.

between France and the United States,[71] Dano composed a "Counterproposition to the Project of M. Gwin" and pressured Maximilian on his financial obligations to France.[72] News of the Mexican Empire's refusal to cede Sonora's mines reached France on July 15. Angered, Napoleon immediately sent dispatches to both Bazaine and Dano, who defensively explained both the reasons they could not implement his instructions and the economic and military pressures that they had already applied.[73]

Demoralized by Maximilian's official rejection, Gwin wrote to Napoleon on the day before he left Mexico for good. Vainly appealing for justice, he complained that Bazaine had refused to protest Maximilian's repudiation because of the "confidential nature" of the subject which could not be publicized "without irreverence and danger." Acknowledging failure, Gwin decided to leave immediately and requested a military escort to Matamoras.[74] After feeling abandoned by two emperors, in 1865 he was imprisoned for over seven months by his native country. Incarcerated at Fort Jackson, he helplessly continued to write the Marquis de Montholon.[75]

71. Montholon to Drouyn de Lhuys, July 14, 1865, extracts ibid., 148-49.
72. Dano to Drouyn de Lhuys, August 29 and July 28, 1865, ibid., 149-54, 183-85. See also enclosure no. 2 of same to same, June 11, 1865 AEF, CP, Mex., vol. 63.
73. Bazaine to the French minister of war, August 27, 1865; and Dano to Drouyn de Lhuys, August 29, 1865, Díaz, *Versión francesa*, IV, 175-76, 183-85. For the many French dispatches on this subject see ibid. This reaction in itself—threats, bluffs, accusations, and involved explanations to the French emperor on the failure to obtain the cession of Sonora's mineral rights for France—would support a separate study.
74. Gwin to his wife and children, June 29, 1865, and Gwin to Napoleon, July 3, 1865, Coleman, "Gwin's Plan," *Overland Monthly* 17 (June 1891): 594, 597; Rippy, "Mexican Projects," p. 315; and W. C. Nunn, *Escape From Reconstruction* (Fort Worth: Leo Potishman Foundation, Texas Christian University, 1956), p. 29.
75. Gwin to Montholon, Fort Jackson, October 15, 1865, Coleman, "Gwin's Plan," *Overland Monthly* 18 (August 1891): 209. Seward, who had served in the Senate with Gwin, was responsible for Gwin's arrest in 1865 and also strongly opposed his release. As late as February, 1867 Seward allegedly had spies or detectives following Gwin who, upon his release, returned to France. William V. Wells to Maximilian, February 14, 1867, HHUSA, Max., karton 141, docs. 13-14. See Coleman, "Gwin and Seward: A Secret Chapter in Ante-Bellum History", *Overland Monthly* 18 (November 1891): 465-71.

William McKendree Gwin's departure from Mexico City on July 4, 1865, had been accompanied by a spate of proclamations and correspondence. As Gwin dejectedly rode toward the Rio Grande, Antonio López de Santa Anna, patriotically condemning Maximilian for ceding Sonora to France, issued a proclamation against the empire.[76] On the basis of Mejía's statement that French forces and Gwin had already left for Sonora, Matías Romero mistakenly concluded that Gwin was in the process of actually effecting his plans in Sonora. Disclosing intercepted correspondence, dated May 16-19, 1865, which, although divulging French support for Gwin was innocuous as far as threats to the United States were concerned, Romero felt obliged to theorize that Gwin had a "presentiment" that his letters would be intercepted. However, the Mexican minister skillfully tried to inflame the United States by pointing out that Gwin planned to amass discontented American citizens on the Mexican frontier. Irritated first by the failure of the Hampton Roads conference and then by the curtailment of recruits for Juárez, Romero tenaciously exploited any possible propaganda against Maximilian.[77]

On July 11, Thomas Corwin wrote Seward, "The Sonora project of Dr. William M. Gwin has been suddenly and finally disposed of."[78] Before Corwin's letter reached Seward, however, he received Romero's correspondence and, on July 13, the secretary of state sternly advised Bigelow that the United States would not tolerate either the French emperor's sanction of the "disloyal" Gwin or the reorganization of Confederates as military and political enemies in northern Mexico.[79] This was the first recrudescence of belligerence toward France since the events of May and June had caused Seward to be conciliatory.

Before this letter arrived in France, Drouyn de Lhuys, on the basis of Maximilian's refusal to cede the mineral rights of Sonora, informed his minister in Washington, "It is firmly resolved not to accept the cession

76. Proclamation of Santa Anna, St. Thomas, July 8, 1865, *House Ex. Doc.,* 39th Cong., 1st sess., vol. 1, pt. 3, ser. 1246, doc. 1, p. 667.
77. Mejía to Romero, July 1, 1865, and Romero to Seward, July 8, 1865, ibid., pp. 511-12.
78. Corwin to Seward, July 11, 1865, NA, State, MD Mex., vol. 30, microcopy 97, roll 31.
79. Seward to Bigelow, July 13, 1865, *House Ex. Doc.,* 39th Cong., 1st sess., vol. 1, pt. 3, ser. 1246, doc. 1, pp. 518-19.

of any portion of Mexican territory, and to decline all proposals for concession of mines in Sonora." Irritated by the Mexican emperor's defiance of France, the French foreign minister exhibited no intimidation by the United States and belligerently continued to advocate settlement of Confederate emigrants in mining districts: "No matter about the details of the Emperor Maximilian's plans; this seems to us the proper time to carry them out."[80] Not yet known in either Washington or Paris, French troops took Hermosillo in July 1865—without a shot being fired.[81]

It is implausible to argue that Maximilian simply bowed to Mexican antagonism toward Gwin as an American. He had consistently opposed the idea of admitting Confederate immigrants anywhere near the northern frontier, but during the same month that he disavowed Gwin, he openly and fully supported the Confederate Mathew Fontaine Maury, to whom he entrusted the development of his colonization program—without French control. Colonization had been encouraged but was not well organized. According to *L'Ere nouvelle* a stumbling block had been the requirements that immigrants become naturalized citizens of Mexico. When Maury was also attacked by the press, Maximilian vigorously defended him. The emperor even provided a subsidy of $10,000 to support founding of an English language weekly newspaper, the *Mexican Times.* Devoted to news about American immigrants, its editor and proprietor was former Confederate brigadier general and governor of Louisiana, Henry W. Allen. The paper was published from September 1865 to November 1866.[82]

Mexican newspapers praised the emperor's stand on Sonora. *El pájaro*

---

80. Drouyn de Lhuys to Montholon, July 20, 1865, ibid., pp. 693-94.
81. Dabbs, *French Army in Mexico,* p. 100.
82. Maury had become a naturalized Mexican citizen. Also naturalized was former Confederate General J.B. Magruder who was to supervise the surveying of land for colonization. Corwin to Seward, October 28, 1865 in *House Ex. Doc.,* 39th Cong., 1st sess., vol 1, pt. 3, ser. 1246, doc. 14, p. 460. Also Romero to Seward, December 12, 1865, ibid., pp. 528-30. For more evidence of prospects of immigration by former Confederates, see Romero to Seward, August 3, 1866 with enclosed documents, in *House Ex. Doc.,* 39th Cong., 2nd sess., vol. 1, pt. 3, ser. 1283, pp. 202-03. See also Blondeel to Rogier, April 19, 1865, AEB, CP, Mex., vol. 1, no. 76 and enclosed *L'Ere nouvelle* for April 13, 1865, as well as Dano to Drouyn de Lhuys, June 18, 1865, AEF, CP, Mex., vol. 63. The best file of the *Mexican Times* is at the library of Louisiana State University at Baton Rouge.

verde, asserting the "sacred right" of Mexico to use Sonora's wealth for its own benefit, contended that the purported cession, creating a French buffer state, would have been viewed by the world as a sign of "impotence and weakness" in the possible confrontation with the United States.[83] Even *L'Ere nouvelle,* the French newspaper in Mexico, admitted that the proposed cession had stimulated dissension and had "put the Emperor in a bad light."[84]

• • •

Shifting his dependency on France to the nebulously proffered friendship of the United States, Maximilian hoped for recognition from Washington—and less reliance on Paris. The French government began making plans to withdraw all their troops for the first time since they had received rumors of the impending Hampton Roads conference.[85] On July 30, 1865, two days before Seward's July 13 dispatch had been presented to the French government, Marshal Jacques L. C. A. Randon, the French minister of war, wrote Marshal Bazaine that Maximilian would be well advised to organize a Mexican army—"for we cannot stay eternally in Mexico."[86] In Europe itself the clouds of war were darkening. Prussia had already defeated Denmark and was on the verge of challenging Austria for control of central Europe. France could hardly afford the Mexican adventure much longer.

As the French made plans to withdraw, the Mexican Empire had no more inducements to offer the United States, and so Seward spoke with

---

83. Hanna and Hanna, "Immigration Movement," p. 238, citing *El pájaro verde,* June 27, 1865.
84. Ibid., citing *L'Ere nouvelle,* June 27, 1865. *L'Ere nouvelle* had been established in August 1864 by E. Masseras, former editor of the New York *Courrier des États Unis.* Ibid., p. 233. However, earlier in the debates about Gwin, even its editor had been imprisoned by Bazaine. McPherson, *William McKendree Gwin,* p. 266.
85. Although the French withdrawal from Mexico is outside the scope of this study, see the following 1865 dispatches for assurances that French troops would not be reduced: Eugénie to Carlota, February 3, 1865; Napoleon to Maximilian, March 1, 1865; Eugénie to Carlota, April 1 and May 31, 1865, relating orders from Napoleon, Corti, *Maximilian,* II, 887-89; 895-96, 908-09; and discussion in the *corps législatif,* Thursday, June 8, 1865, *Le Moniteur Universel,* June 9, 1865.
86. Randon to Bazaine, July 30, 1865, Bazaine Archives, vol. 13, f. 2551-53.

increasing directness. Bigelow dutifully reported the intercepted Gwin letters and Seward's July 13 dispatch to Drouyn de Lhuys on August 1, 1865.[87] Six days later the French foreign minister heatedly responded that the French emperor rejected such an arrogant and threatening communication.[88] Bigelow, thoroughly intimidated, wrote Seward, "The sensitiveness betrayed by his Excellency upon this subject has determined me to defer any rejoinder until I have had time to hear from you."[89] Bitterly informing Montholon of the offensive correspondence from Seward which he had answered "by the Emperor's command," Drouyn de Lhuys seethed at the supercilious attitude of the United States which, in their war with Mexico, had "exercised the rights of victory in all their plenitude by annexing a new State." He then admitted, "We yielded to a necessity of the same nature as that which had, at another epoch, conducted the American arms to the capital of Mexico."[90]

Then Franco-American diplomatic dispatches became more subdued. Confessing to Bigelow that Gwin had appeared to be an energetic man, Drouyn de Lhuys diplomatically denied that the emperor had known him.[91] And Seward expressed regret that he had antagonized the French foreign minister.[92]

Meanwhile, Franco-Mexican relations became more strained. Marshal Randon, demanding the return of French troops, impatiently wrote to Bazaine, "The Mexican Government must be thinking that we will sacrifice our own interests for theirs."[93] Maximilian had successfully defied the French, thereby losing their support. At his trial in 1867, he futilely reminded Mexicans that he had defended their territory and had retained Sonora and its mines for Mexico.[94]

---

87. Bigelow to Drouyn de Lhuys, August 1, 1865, Bigelow, *Retrospections,* III, 122-31.
88. Drouyn de Lhuys to Bigelow, August 7, 1865, ibid., p. 145.
89. Bigelow to Seward, August 10, 1865, ibid., p. 147.
90. Drouyn de Lhuys to Montholon, August 17, 1865, *House Ex. Doc.,* 39th Cong., 1st sess., vol. 1, pt. 3, ser. 1246, doc. 1, p. 694-95.
91. Bigelow to Seward, August 31, 1865, Bigelow, *Retrospections,* III, 165-68.
92. Seward to Bigelow, August 24, 1865, ibid., pp. 182-83; and Eugénie to Carlota, September 28, 1865, Corti, *Maximilian,* II, 919-20.
93. Randon to Bazaine, August 31, 1865, Bazaine Archives, vol. 14, f. 2608-09.
94. Samuel Siegfried Karl Basch, *Erinnerungen aus Mexico* (Leipzig: Verlag von Dunder & Humblot, 1868), p. 229. See appendix of Basch for Maximilian's hand-written defense notes.

Although infuriated by Maximilian's duplicity and ingratitude, Napoleon had achieved the major goals which had originally stimulated the French intervention in Mexico. Despite the denial of formal control of Sonora's mines, an enormous amount of silver had poured into the French treasury, enabling it to cope with the crises caused by the influx of gold in the 1850s. Mexican silver had arrested the flow of silver from France and had also paid for the desperately needed cotton from India. During the five-year period preceding French intervention in Mexico, from 1857 to 1861, the French had received an average of only £9,221 per year in Mexican bullion and specie. When the French were in Mexico, this amount increased dramatically: from 1862 to 1867, they obtained a staggering average of £ 373,019 per year—more than forty times their previous annual amount, to the outrage of the United States and Great Britain whom France had replaced as the major recipient of Mexican silver.[95]

Napoleon III's intervention in Mexico was not quixotic. It was based on economic necessity, an acute need for silver. As Eugénie herself, years later, pragmatically asked, "Do you suppose there was nothing but piety in the crusades?"[96]

---

95. "Values of the Imports of Merchandise and Bullion into England, France, and the United States, from Mexico, 1857-1871," *Hansard's: Currency*, appendix, p. 708. For the improving silver situation during 1865 at the Bank of France, see *Le Moniteur Universel* for January 12, February 2, March 24, May 12,19,26, June 1,8,23 and 30. Also on the replenishing of the Bank of France's silver stocks in the mid and late 1860s see "Report on the Fall of the Price of Silver", *Hansard's: Currency*, VI, p. 53.
96. Eugénie-Paléologue interview, December 27, 1903, Maurice Paléologue, *The Tragic Empress: Intimate Conversations with the Empress Eugénie, 1901 to 1911*, trans. Hamish Miles (London: Harpers, 1928), p. 84.

Epilogue

Napoleon's intervention in Mexico had been heralded in mid 1864 as his best enterprise, the one that would be most "applauded" for the benefits it would bestow upon the entire world.[1] Contrary to this expectation, historians for more than a century have regarded it as the French emperor's greatest folly, an irrational and imperialistic move. It engendered the hostility of the United States, the animosity of Mexico, the bitterness of Austria, the irritation of Great Britain and Spain, and the antagonism of Frenchmen.

Fear of French intervention in Mexico existed even when Napoleon was a political prisoner at Ham, two and one-half years before he became president of the Second French Republic.[2] Thus the idea was not novel. Yet the world, wary of a Bonaparte, was perplexed by the cause of such a move in 1861. And Napoleon, viewed by a contemporary as permitting "no light or shadow of his design to fall upon the public mind until it suits him," kept his silence.[3]

A nation's vulnerability is best not publicized. The flood of gold from America and Australia in the 1850s had caused French silver to become precious. It was hoarded, melted down, and exported. Napoleon urgently needed silver to provide balance to his bimetallic monetary standard, to supply the substance for small coins, to replenish silver bank reserves depleted by the scarcity, to restore confidence in the French monetary system which had been adopted by neighboring countries, and to offer assurance of stability to traditionally oriented bankers and financiers. These were the vexing problems of the 1850s as the French count Gaston Raoul de Raousset-Boulbon and the Swiss banker Jean Baptiste Jecker were trying to obtain the silver

---

1. Robert Hogarth Patterson, "The Napoleonic Idea in Mexico," *Blackwood's Edinburgh Magazine* 96 (July 1864): 72.
2. Buchanan to Slidell, March 12, 1846, Manning, VIII, doc. 3255, 189-92.
3. "Maximilian," *Blackwood's Edinburgh Magazine* 102 (August 1867): 235.

mines of Sonora. Raousset-Boulbon and Jecker alerted Napoleon to sources for his desperately needed silver, allegedly wasted in a remote Mexican state, territory coveted by the United States and scantily but primarily mined by British investors. And throughout this decade, Mexican monarchists appealed to him for help in establishing order and security for Mexico.

Having been buffeted by problems caused by the influx of gold, Napoleon's need for silver became crucial in the 1860s. When the American Civil War cut off his major source of cotton, he quickly cast about for alternative supplies. The readiest source was in India, which accepted only silver as payment for the raw cotton so vital to France. The alternative was grim. Devastated textile manufacturers, anxious investors, and unemployed workers were an awesome and potential force of unrest, and Napoleon was determined to avoid a revolution. He had to have cotton immediately, and he had to obtain silver for payment.

This he did. With French troops in Mexico, he quickly pushed on, despite Spanish and British opposition, and obstinately maintained that the Mexican Empire was responsible for reimbursing the expedition's expenses. These, Napoleon suggested, could be paid for by a lien on the mines of Sonora. To obtain this concession and to promote the productivity of these mines, he relied on his minister to Mexico, the Marquis de Montholon, and an American entrepreneur, William McKendree Gwin. Frustrated by Maximilian, Montholon and Gwin eventually failed in their efforts to carry out the French emperor's instructions. Nonetheless, Mexican silver in massive quantities was channeled to France.

Thus, Mexican silver paid for cotton from India and, by 1865, ended the crippling excess of French silver exports. Although thwarted by the Emperor Maximilian in obtaining Sonora's mines, Napoleon had accomplished his primary objective. The French intervention in Mexico was not his greatest folly. It was instead, for France, a monetary and economic success.

A Selected Bibliography

Unpublished Primary Material

Austria. Vienna. Haus-, Hof-, und Staatsarchiv, Archiv Kaiser Maximilians von Mexico,1862-65. Photostatic copies in Library of Congress.

Bazaine Archives, 1862-67. 26 fol. vols., 5265 leaves. Latin American Library, University of Texas, Austin, Texas.

Belgium. Brussels. Archives du ministère des affaires étrangères et du commerce extérieure, Correspondance politique, Légations, France, vol. 22; Mexique, vol. 1, Série générale reliée, Etats-Unis, vol. 6; and Papiers Beyens, Film no. 260, dossier no. 341.

Bigelow Papers, 62 vols., 38 boxes. New York Public Library, New York City, N.Y.

France. Paris. Archives du ministère des affaires étrangères, Correspondance politique, Mexique, vol. 63; and Etats-Unis, vol. 133.

Great Britain. London. Public Record office. Foreign Office Series, especially nos. 27, 50 and 519.

Maximilian and Carlota Collection, Rare Book Room, Fondren Library, Rice University, Houston, Texas. This includes Éloin correspondence.

Pinart, Alphonse. Documents for the History of Sonora: Extracts from Manuscripts and Printed Matter in the Collection of Mons. Alphonse Pinart. MSS in the Bancroft Library, University of California, Berkeley, California. Mexican MSS, nos. 286-92. This rich collection includes the following newspapers: *El Nacional* (Ures, Sonora) 1853-54; *El Sonorense* (Ures, Sonora) 1851-52; *Integridad Nacional* (Mexico City) 1854-56; and *La Voz del Pueblo* (Ures, Sonora) 1852.

United States. Washington. National Archives, Department of State. Dispatches from United States Ministers to Mexico (1823-1906), vol. 28 (December 21, 1859 – February 5, 1862); and vol. 30 (June 26, 1863 – July 31, 1867), microcopy 97, rolls 29 and 31.

Published Government Documents

Austria

Reichs-Gesetz-Blatt für das Kaiserthum Oesterreich, Wien, April 14, 1865, pp. 31-48. *Convention zwischen Oesterreich und Mexico vom 19 October 1864.* Rare Book Room, Fondren Library, Rice University, Houston, Texas.

Belgium

Compte rendu des discussions de la commision réunie par M.J. Malou, Ministre des Finances, à Bruxelles, Octobre-Novembre 1873, pour examiner avec lui des diverses questions monétaire. Bruxelles, 1874.

Lefêvre, Eugéne. *Documents officiels recueillis dans la secrétaire privés de Maximilien. Histoire de l'intervention française au Mexique.* 2 vols. Bruxelles, 1869.

Malou, M.J. *Documents relatifs à la question monétaire, recueillis et publiés en fascicules.* Bruxelles, 1874.

Rapport déposé par M. le Ministre des Finances a la chambre des Représentants. Séance du 20 Août, 1859, Question monétaire, no. 18. Bruxelles, 1859.

France

Documents relatifs à la question monétaire, Procès-verbaux et rapport de la commission monétaire de 1867 relatifs à la question de l'étalon. Paris, 1868. *Enquête sur les principes et les faits généraux qui régissent la circulation monétaire et fiduciaire.* 6 vols. Paris: Conseil supérieur de l'agriculture, du commerce, et de l'industrie, 1869. Vol. 6.

Enquête sur la question monétaire, Décembre 1869-Août 1871. Paris: Conseil supérieur de l'agriculture, du commerce, et de l'industrie, 1872.

Montluc, Léon de, ed. *Armand de Montluc, correspondance de Juárez et de Montluc, ancien consul général du Mexique, accompagnée de nombreuses lettres de personnages politiques, relatives à l'expédition du Mexique.* Paris: G. Charpentier et cie, 1885.

Poulet-Malassis, A. *Papiers secrets et correspondance du Second Empire. Réimpression complète de l'édition de l'imprimérie nationale, annotée et augmentée de nombreuses pièces publiées à l'étranger, et recueilliés par A. Poulet-Malassis.* 3rd ed. Paris: Ghio et cie, 1873.

Rapport de la commission chargée d'étudier la question monétaire. Documents relatifs à la question monétaire. Paris: Ministère des finances, Enquête de 1858.

Rapport de la commission chargée d'étudier la question de l'étalon monétaire. Paris: Ministère des finances, 1869.

Great Britain

Parliament. *Hansard's Parliamentary Papers, 3rd ser.* (House of Commons), *Report from the Select Committee on the Depreciation of Silver with Evidence and Papers from Representatives Abroad, Monetary Policy: Currency,* vol. 6, 1876. An extensive presentation of critically important economic and fiscal data.

Mexico

Comisión Científica de Pachuca, 1864. México: J. M. Andrade y F. Escalante, 1865.

Decrees of the Mexican Constitutional Republican Government, Inviting American Emigrants to Settle in the Republic of Mexico. San Francisco, California: Imprenta de "La Voz de Méjico," 1865. Copy in the Huntington Library, San Marino, California.

Diaz, Lilia, trans. *Version francesa de Mexico: Informes diplomaticos.* 4 vols. Mexico: El Colegio de Mexico, 1963-67.

García, Genaro, ed. *Colección de documentos inéditos ó muy raros para la historia de México.* 30 vols. México: Librería de la Vda. de Ch. Bouret, 1908-10. Vol. 16.

Paredes, Mariano. *Proyectos de leyes sobre colonización y comercio en el estado de Sonora, presentados a la Cámera de Diputados, por el representante de aquel estado, en la sesion extraordinario del dia 16 de Agosto de 1850.* Mexico: Imprenta de I. Cumplido, 1850.

Segura, José Sebastián, ed. *Boletín de las leyes del Imperio mexicano ó sea Código de la restauración.* 4 vols. México: Imprenta literaria, 1863-65. Vol. 1.

Torre Villar, Ernesto de la, et al., eds. *Historia documental de Mexico.* 2 vols. Mexico: Universidad Nacional Autonóma de Mexico, 1964. Vol. 2.

Weckmann, Luis, ed. *Las relaciónes franco-mexicanas.* 2 vols. Mexico: Secretaria de relaciones exteriores, 1961-62. Vol. 2.

United States

Manning, William R., ed. *Diplomatic Correspondence of the United States: Inter-American Affairs, 1831-1860.* 10 vols. Washington: Carnegie Endowment for International Peace, 1937. Vols. 6, 8 and 9.

Richardson, James D., ed. *A Compilation of the Messages and Papers of the Confederacy, Including the Diplomatic Correspondence, 1861-1865.* 10 vols. Washington: Washington Post Co., 1905. Vol. 6.

Congress. *Congressional Globe.* 32nd Cong., 2nd sess.; 33rd Cong., 1st sess.; 35th Cong., 1st sess.; 37th Cong., 3rd sess.; and 38th Cong., 1st sess.

Congress. House. *House Executive Documents.* 35th Cong., 1st sess.; 37th Cong., 2nd and 3rd sess.; 39th Cong., 1st and 2nd sess.; 40th Cong., 1st sess; and 41st Cong., 2nd sess. These publications, organized by document and serial set numbers, along with the companion *Senate Executive Documents,* encompass a vast amount of important diplomatic correspondence, much of it anticipating later documentary publications.

Congress. Senate. *Senate Executive Documents.* 33rd Cong., 2nd sess.; 38th Cong., 2nd sess.; 39th Cong., 1st sess.; and 40th Cong., 1st sess.

Congress. Senate. *Senate Journal,* 35th Cong., 1st sess.

Congress. Senate. *Senate Reports.* 44th Cong., 2nd sess.., vol. 5, pt. 1, ser. set 1738, *Report of the United States Monetary Commission,* Washington, 1876.

Department of Commerce. *Historical Statistics of the United States, Colonial Times to 1957.* Washington, 1960.

Department of State. *Diplomatic Correspondence.* 39th Cong., 1st sess. Washington, 1865.

Statutes at Large. Vol. 9, pt. 2 (December 1845 – March 1851), "Treaty of Peace, Friendship, Limits, and Settlement with the Republic of Mexico," February 2, 1848; and vol. 10, pt. 2 (December 1851-March 1855), "Treaty with Mexico," December 30, 1853.

Other Contemporary Source Material

Académie des sciences. *Comptes rendus hebdomadaires des séances de l'académie des sciences.* Paris, 1847. Vol. 25.

Annuaire des Deux Mondes. Paris, 1851-53.

Bartlett, John Russell. *Personal Narrative of Explorations and Incidents in Texas, New Mexico, California, Sonora, and Chihuahua.* 2 vols. New York: D. Appleton, 1854. Vol. 2.

Basch, Samuel Siegfried Karl. *Erinnerungen aus Mexico.* Leipzig: Verlag von Duncker & Humblot, 1868.

Baudrillart, Henri. "Des crises monétaires et de la question de l'or." *Journal des économistes,* 2nd ser., 7 (July-September 1855): 360-89.

_____. "Chronique économique." *Journal des économistes,* 2nd ser., 2 (October– December 1856): 474 et seq.

Beyens, Napoleon Eugéne, *Le Second Empire, vu par un diplomate belge.* 2 vols. Paris, Plon-Nourrit et cie, 1925.

Bordet, H. *L'Or et L'Argent en 1864.* Paris: Guillaumin et cie, 1864.

Box, Jim. "The Mines of Northern Mexico." *Knickerbocker Magazine* 57 (June 1861): 577-87.

Bigelow, John. *Retrospections of an Active Life.* 3 vols. New York: Baker & Taylor, 1909. Vol. 2.

Blanchot, Charles. *Mémoires, L'Intervention Française au Mexique.* 3 vols. Paris: Émile Nourry, 1911. Vol. 2.

Case, Lynn M. *French Opinion on the United States and Mexico, 1860-1867: Extracts from the Reports of the Procureurs Généraux.* New York: D. Appleton-Century, 1936.

Charnay, Désiré. *Les anciennes villes du Nouveau Monde: voyages d'exploration au Mexique et dans L'Amérique Centrale, 1857-1882.* Paris, 1885.

Cherbuliez, A. E. "La question monétaire en Suisse." *Journal des économistes,* 2nd ser., 25 (January-March 1860): 40-58.

Chevalier, Michel. *De la baisse probable de l'or, des conséquences commerciales et sociales qu'elle peut avoir et des mesures qu'elle provoque.* Paris: Capelle, 1859.

Coleman, Evan J. "Senator Gwin's Plan for the Colonization of Sonora." *Overland Monthly,* 2nd ser., 17 (May 1891): 497-519; 17 (June 1891): 593-607; and 18 (August 1891): 203-13. Important documents and correspondence.

_____. "Gwin and Seward: A Secret Chapter in Ante-Bellum History." *Overland Monthly,* 2nd ser., 18 (November 1891): 465-71.

_____. "Dr. Gwin and Judge Black on Buchanan." *Overland Monthly* 2nd ser., 19 (January 1892): 87-92.

Coppey, Hypolite. *El Conde Raousset-Boulbon en Sonora.* Trans. by Alberto Cubillas. México: Librería de Manuel Porrua, S.A., 1962. Reprint of 1855 edition.

Corti, Count Egon Caesar. *Maximilian and Charlotte of Mexico.* Trans. by Catherine Alison Phillips. 2 vols. New York: Alfred A. Knopf, 1929. A basic pioneering work, reproduces a host of important documents.

Dommartin, Hippolyte du Pasquier de. *Les États-Unis et le Mexique: l'intérêt européen dans l'Amérique du nord.* Paris: Guillaumin, 1852.

"The Empire of Mexico." *Quarterly Review* 115 (April 1864): 348-81.

Faulk, Odie B., ed. "A Colonization Plan for Northern Sonora, 1850." *New Mexico Historical Review* 44 (October 1969): 293-314.

_____, trans. and ed. "Projected Mexican Colonies in the Borderlands, 1852." *Journal of Arizona History* 10 (Summer 1969): 115-28.

_____, trans. and ed. "Projected Mexican Military Colonies for the Borderlands, 1848." *Journal of Arizona History* 9 (Spring 1968): 39-47.

Fontenay, R. de. "La question monétaire." *Journal des économistes,* 2nd ser., 26 (April-June 1860): 391-406.

Gardiner, C. Harvey, ed. *Mexico, 1825-1828: The Journal and Correspondence of Edward Thornton Tayloe.* Chapel Hill: University of North Carolina Press, 1959.

Gaulot, Paul. *La vérité sur l'expédition du Mexique, d'après les documents inédits de Ernest Lovet, payeur en chef du corps expéditionnaire.* 3 vols. Paris: P. Ollendorff, 1890.

Gwin, William McKendree. "Memoirs of Hon. William M. Gwin." William Henry Ellison, ed. *California Historical Society Quarterly* 19 (March-December 1940): 1-26; 157-84; 256-77; 344-67.

Herring, Partricia R. "A Plan for the Colonization of Sonora's Northern Frontier: The Paredes Proyectos of 1850." *Journal of Arizona History* 10 (Summer 1969): 103-14.

Hidalgo, José María. *Proyectos de monarquia en Mexico.* México: F. Vázques, 1904.

Horn, J. E. "La crise monétaire." *Journal des économistes,* 2nd ser., 31 (July-September 1861): 5-20.

_____. "Bulletin financier de l'étranger." *Journal des économistes,* 2nd ser., 35 (July-September 1862): 321-25.

_____. "Situation des finances Italiennes." *Journal des économistes,* 3rd ser., 1 (January-March 1866): 274-311.

Humboldt, Alexander von. *Essai politique sur le royaume de la nouvelle espagne.* 5 vols. Paris: Chez F. Schoell, 1811.

Journal de la Société des Américanistes de Paris. 10 vols., Paris: 1903-13. Vol. 10.

Kératry, Comte Emile de. *La créance Jecker, les indemnités françaises at les emprunts Mexicains.* Paris: Librairie internationale, 1868.

_____. *L'Empereur Maximilien: Son élévation et sa chute.* Amsterdam: L. Van Bakkenes, 1867.

Kinnaird, Lawrence, ed. *The Frontiers of New Spain: Nicolás de Lafora's Description, 1766-1768.* Berkeley, California: Quivira Society, 1958.

Lachapelle, Alfred Comte de. *Le comte de Raousset-Boulbon et l'expédition de la Sonore: correspondance, souvenirs et ouvres inédites.* Paris: E. Dentu, 1859.

Lambertie, Charles de. *Le drame de Sonora, l'état de Sonora, M. le comte de Raousset-Boulbon et M. Charles de Pindray.* Paris: Ledoyen, 1855.

Levasseur, Emile. *La question de l'or; les mines de Californie et d'Australie, les anciennes mines d'or et d'argent, leur production, la distribution et l'emploi: des métaux precieux, l'influence des nouvelles mines d'or sur la société, leur avenir, les problèmes qu'elles soulèvent, les réformes qu'elles provoquent.* Paris: Guillaumin, et cie, 1858.

London Economist. 1861.

Lower California Colonization Co., to Jabob P. Leese and Others. No place or exact date. Original in the Huntington Library, San Marino, California.

The Lower California Mining Co. Prospectus: *Grants and Concessions from Mexico, Documents and Reports.* New York: "The Stockholder" Print, 1865. Copy in the Huntington Library, San Marino, California.

Madelène, Henri de la. *Le comte Gaston de Raousset-Boulbon: sa vie et ses aventures d'après ses papiers et sa correspondance.* Paris: Charpentier, 1876. 1st ed., 1856. 2nd ed., 1859.

Malte-Brun, Victor Adolphe. *La Sonora et ses mines. Equisse géographique.* Paris: Arthus Bertrand, 1864.

"Maximilian." *Blackwood's Edinburgh Magazine* 102 (August 1867): 235.

McCulloch, J. R. *A Select Collection of Scarce and Valuable Tracts and Other Publications, on Paper Currency and Banking.* London: 1857.

Mexican Times, Mexico City, 1865. The most complete file is at the Louisiana State University Library, Baton Rouge, Louisiana.

"Mexico, by Baron Humboldt." *Catholic World* 7 (1868): 328-36.

Miles, Carlota, ed. and trans. *Almada of Alamos: The Diary of Don Bartolomé.* Tucson: Arizona Silhouettes, 1962.

"The Mines of Santa Eulalia, Chihuahua." *Harper's New Monthly Magazine* 35 (November 1867): 681-702.

Le Moniteur Universel, Paris, 1862 and 1865.

"Monthly Record of Current Events." *Harper's New Monthly Magazine* 19 (December 1851):124.

Mowry, Sylvester. *Arizona and Sonora: The Geography, History, and Resources of the Silver Region of North America.* 3rd ed. rev. New York: Harper & Brothers, 1864.

Murray, Robert Hammond, ed. and trans. *Maximilian, Emperor of Mexico: Memoirs of His Private Secretary José Luis Blasio.* New Haven: Yale University Press, 1934.

"My Mexican Mines." *Harper's New Monthly Magazine* 35 (September 1867): 456-62. An anonymous article by a disillusioned investor.

New York Times, December 15, 22, 24, 1852; and January 10, 1853.

Niox, Gustave Léon. *L'Expédition du Mexique, 1861-67. Récit politique et militaire.* Paris: Librairie militaire de J. Dumoine, 1874.

"Notice sur deux nouveaux minéraux découverts à Culebras, au Mexique." *Annales des sciences naturelles* 14 (December 1827): 371-74.

Ollivier, Émile. *La intervencion francesa y el imperio de Maximiliano en Mexico.* 2nd ed. México: Ediciones Centenario, 1963.

Paléologue, Maurice. *The Tragic Empress: Intimate Conversations with the Empress Eugénie, 1901 to 1911.* Translated by Hamish Miles. London, [Harpers, 1928].

Parieu, E. de. "La question monétaire française." *Journal des économistes,* 2nd ser., 2 (October-December 1856): 474 et seq.

Patterson, Robert Hogarth. "The Napoleonic Idea in Mexico." *Blackwood's Edinburgh Magazine* 96 (July 1864): 72-83.

Pfefferkorn, Ignaz. *Sonora: A Description of the Province.* Trans. by Theodore E. Treutlein. Albuquerque: University of New Mexico Press, 1949. First published in two volumes as *Beschreibung der landschaft Sonora* at Köln am Rheine, 1794-95.

"The Plot of the Mexican Drama." *Eclectic Magazine,* n.s., 6 (November 1867): 528-44.

Pollard, S., and C. Holmes, eds. *Documents of European Economic History.* Vol. 1, *The Process of Industrialization, 1750-1870.* [London]: Edward Arnold, [1968].

"Produit du Mexique en or et en argent monnayés." *Annales des sciences naturelles* 26 (October 1829): 113-14.

"Report of the United Mining Association, March, 1837." *Philosophical Magazine* 2 (July 1827): 70-76.

Report of Frederick Brunckow to a Committee of the Stockholders of the Sonora Exploring & Mining Co. upon the History, Resources, and Prospects of the Company in Arizona. Cincinnati: Railroad Record, 1859.

"Review of Alexander de Humboldt's Travels." *Quarterly Review* 21(1819): 320-52.

Revue des cours scientifiques de la France et des l'étranger. Paris, 1864—. Vols. 1-3.

Robina, Lucia de. *Reconciliacion de México y Francia, 1870-1880.* Archivo Histórico Diplomatico Mexicano. 2nd ser., no. 16. México: Secretaría de Relaciones Exteriores, 1963.

Romero, Matías. *Historia de las intrigas europeas que ocasionaron la intervención francesa en México.* México: Imprenta del gobierno, J. M. Sandoval, 1868.

_____. *Mexico and the United States: A Study of Subjects Affecting their Political, Commercial, and Social Relations, made with a View to their Promotion.* New York: G. P. Putnam's Sons, 1898.

Saint-Clair-Duport. *De la production des métaux précieux au Mexique, considérée dans ses rapports avec la géologie, la métallurgie et l'économie politique.* Paris: F. Didot frères, 1843.

Sartorius, Carl. *Mexico About 1850.* Stuttgart: F. A. Brockhaus Komm.-Gesch. G.M.B.H., Abt. Antiquarium, 1961. Translation of the Darmstadt, 1858, edition.

"State and Prospects of Mexico, 1845." *Eclectic Magazine* 6 (December 1845): 433-51.

Stevenson, Sara Yorke. *Maximilian in Mexico: A Woman's Reminiscences of the French Intervention, 1862-1867.* New York: Century, 1899.

Stone, Charles P. "Notes on the State of Sonora." *Historical Magazine* 5 (June 1861): 161-69.

Temperly, Harold, and Lillian M. Penson, eds. *Foundations of British Foreign Policy: From Pitt (1792) to Salisbury (1902).* London: Frank Cass, 1966.

Villa, Eduardo W. *Historia de Estado de Sonora.* 2nd ed. Hermosillo, Sonora: Editorial Sonora, 1851.

Ward, H[enry] G[eorge]. *Mexico in 1827.* 2 vols. London: Henry Colburn, 1828.

Secondary Studies

Adams, Ephraim Douglass. *Great Britain and the American Civil War.* New York: Russell & Russell, 1958.

Arnaiz y Freg, Arturo, and Claude Battaillon, eds. *La intervencion francesa y el imperio de Maximiliano: Cien años después 1862-1962.* México: Asociación Mexicana de Historiadores; Instituto Francés de América Latina, 1965.

Bagwell, Philip S., and G. E. Mingay. *Britain and America, 1850-1939: A Study of Economic Change.* London: Routledge & Kegan Paul, 1970.

Bancroft, Hubert Howe. *History of Arizona and New Mexico.* San Francisco: History Company, 1889.

_____. *History of California, 1848-1859.* 7 vols. San Francisco: History Company, 1888. Vol. 6.

_____. *History of Mexico, 1824-1861.* 6 vols. San Francisco: A. L. Bancroft, 1885. Vols. 3-6.

_____. *History of the North Mexican States and Texas.* 2 vols. San Francisco: A. L. Bancroft, 1884.

Barker, Nancy Nichols. *The French Experience in Mexico, 1821 – 1861: A History of Constant Misunderstanding.* Chapel Hill: University of North Carolina Press, 1979.

_____. "The Duke of Morny and the Affair of the Jecker Bonds." *French Historical Studies* 6 (Fall 1970): 555-61.

136 • *Napoleon III and Mexican Silver*

_____. "The Empress Eugénie and the Origin of the Mexican Venture." *The Historian,* XXII, 1 (1959): 9-23.

Bemis, Samuel Flagg, ed. *The American Secretaries of State and Their Diplomacy.* 10 vols. New York: Alfred A. Knopf, 1928. Vol. 7.

Benson, Nettie Lee. "Mexican Monarchists, 1823-1867." A paper presented March 23, 1973 at the Southwest Social Science Association, Dallas, Texas.

Blattner, Helen Harland. *The Political Career of William McKendree Gwin.* M.A. thesis, University of California at Berkeley, 1914.

Blumberg, Arnold. *The Diplomacy of the Mexican Empire, 1863-1867.* Philadelphia: American Philosophical Society, 1971. Superb study with fine bibliography.

Blumenthal, Henry. *A Reappraisal of Franco-American Relations, 1830-1871.* Chapel Hill: University of North Carolina Press, 1959.

Bock, Carl H. *Prelude to Tragedy: The Negotiation and Breakdown of the Tripartite Convention of London, October 31, 1861.* Philadelphia: University of Pennsylvania Press, 1966. Thorough study, excellent bibliography.

Cairnes, J. E. *Essays in Political Economy.* London: Macmillan, 1873.

Calcott, Wilfrid Hardy. *Santa Anna: The Story of an Enigma Who Once Was Mexico.* Norman: University of Oklahoma Press, 1936.

Cameron, Rondo. *France and the Economic Development of Europe, 1800-1914: Conquests of Peace and Seeds of War.* Princeton: Princeton University Press, 1961.

_____, et al. *Banking in the Early Stages of Industrialization: A Study in Comparative Economic History.* New York: Oxford University Press, 1967.

Case, Lynn M., and Warren F. Spencer. *The United States and France: Civil War Diplomacy.* Philadelphia: University of Pennsylvania Press, 1970. Thoroughly documented study.

Clapham, J. H. *The Economic Development of France and Germany, 1815-1914.* 4th ed. Cambridge: University Press, 1961.

Corral, Ramón. *Obras históricas: Reseña histórica del Estado de Sonora, 1856-1877.* Hermosillo, México: Biblioteca sonorense de geografía e historia, 1959.

Cosío Villegas, Daniel. *Historia moderna de México: La república restaurada.* 3 vols. México: Editorial Hermes, 1955. Vol. 2, *La vida economica.*

Crespo y Martínez, Gilberto. *México: industria mineria, estudio de su evolución.* México: Oficina tip. de la Secretaría de fomento, 1903.

Crouzet, F., W. H. Chaloner, and W. M. Stern, eds. *Essays in European Economic History, 1789-1914.* New York: St. Martin's Press, 1969.

Dabbs, Jack Autrey. *The French Army in Mexico, 1861-1867: A Study in Military Government*. The Hague: Mouton, 1963.

Dargens, André, and Fernand J. Tomiche. *L'or et son avenir*. [Paris]: Librairie Hachette, 1967.

Dawson, Daniel. *The Mexican Adventure*. London: G. Bell & Sons, 1935.

Del Mar, Alexander. *A History of the Precious Metals: From the Earliest Times to the Present*. London: G. Bell & Sons, 1880.

Delord, Taxile. *Histoire du second empire: 1848-1869*. 6 vols. Paris: Librairie Germer Baillière, 1869-75. Vol. 3.

Desternes, Suzanne, and Henriette Chandet. *Maximilien et Charlotte*. Paris: Librairie Académique Perrin, 1964.

Díaz, Vicente Fuentes. *La intervencion europa en México, 1861-62*. México: n.p. 1962.

Duchesne, Albert. *L'expédition des volontaires belges au Mexique: 1864-1867*. 2 vols. Brussels: Musée Royal de l'armée et d'histoire militaire, 1967-68.

Dunbier, Roger. *The Sonoran Desert: Its Geography, Economy, and People*. Tucson: University of Arizona Press, 1968.

Dunham, Arthur Louis. *The Anglo-French Treaty of Commerce of 1860 and the Progress of the Industrial Revolution in France*. Ann Arbor: University of Michigan Press, 1930.

Ellstaetter, Karl. *The Indian Silver Currency: An Historical and Economic Study*. Trans. by J. Laurence Laughlin. Chicago: University of Chicago Press, 1895.

Feavearyear, Sir Albert. *The Pound Sterling: A History of English Money*. 2nd ed. rev., by E. Victor Morgan. Oxford: Clarendon Press, 1963.

Fisher, H. A. L. *Bonapartism: Six Lectures Delivered in the University of London*. London: Oxford University Press, 1908.

Fohlen, Claude. *L'industrie textile au temps du Second Empire*. Paris: Librairie Plon, [1956].

_____. "Crise textile et troubles sociaux: le Nord à la fin du Second Empire." *Revue du Nord* (1953): 107-23.

Garner, Richard L. "Long-Term Silver Mining Trends in Spanish America: A Comparative Analysis of Peru and Mexico." *American Historical Review* 93 (October 1988): 898-935.

Gayer, Arthur D., William W. Rostow et al. *The Growth and Fluctuation of the British Economy, 1790-1850*. 2 vols. Oxford: Clarendon Press, 1953. Vol. 1.

Gilmore, N. Ray. "Henry George Ward, British Publicist for Mexican Mines." *Pacific Historical Review* 32 (February 1963): 35-47.

Haight, Frank Arnold. *A History of French Commercial Policies.* NewYork: Macmillan, 1941.

Hale, Charles A. *Mexican Liberalism in the Age of Mora, 1821-1853.* New Haven: Yale University Press, 1968.

Hammond, M. B. *The Cotton Industry.* New York: MacMillan, 1897.

Hanna, Alfred Jackson, and Kathryn Abbey Hanna. *Napoleon III and Mexico.* Chapel Hill: University of North Carolina Press, 1971. A fine study with a superb bibliography.

_____. "The Immigration Movement of the Intervention and Empire as Seen Through the Mexican Press." *Hispanic American Historical Review* 27 (May 1947): 220-46.

Hanna, Kathryn Abbey. "Incidents of the Confederate Blockade." *Journal of Southern History* 11 (February 1945): 214-29.

_____. The Roles of the South in the French Intervention in Mexico." *Journal of Southern History* 20 (February 1954): 3-21.

Harmon, George D. "Confederate Migration to Mexico." *Hispanic American Historical Review* 17 (November 1937): 458-87.

Hawtrey, R. G. *The Gold Standard in Theory and Practice.* 5th ed. London: Longmans, Green, 1947. First published, 1927.

Henderson, W. O. *The Lancashire Cotton Famine, 1861-1865.* Manchester: University Press, 1934.

Juglar, Clément. *Des crises commerciales et de leur retour périodique en France, en Angleterre et aux États-Unis.* 2nd ed. Paris: Guillaumin et cie, 1889.

Labrousse, Camille Ernest. *La crise de l'économie française: à la fin de l'ancien régime et au début de la révolution.* Paris: Presses Universitaires de France, 1944.

La Gorce, Pierre de. *Histoire du second empire.* 12th ed. 7 vols. Paris: Plon-Nourrit et cie, 1874. Vol. 4.

Landes, D. "The Old Bank and the New: The Financial Revolution of the Nineteenth Century," in F. Crouzet, et al., *Essays,* 112-23.

Laughlin, J. Laurence. *The History of Bimetallism in the United States.* New York: D. Appleton, 1892.

Lefebvre, Georges. *Napoleon.* Henry F. Stockhold, trans. 2 vols. New York: Columbia University Press, 1969. Vol. 1, *From 18 Brumaire to Tilsit, 1799-1807.*

Lévy, Robert. *Histoire économique de l'industrie cotonnière en Alsace: étude de sociologie descriptif.* Paris: Alcan, 1912.

Lynn, Vela Leatrice. *The Political Career of Teodosio Lares, 1848-1867.* Ph.D. dissertation, University of Texas, 1951.

McPherson, Hallie Mae. *William McKendree Gwin: Expansionist.* Ph.D. dissertation, University of California at Berkeley, 1931.

Nunn, W. C. *Escape from Reconstruction.* Fort Worth: Leo Potishman Foundation, Texas Christian University, 1956.

Owsley, Frank Lawrence. *King Cotton Diplomacy: Foreign Relations of the Confederate States of America.* 2nd ed. rev. Chicago: University of Chicago Press, 1959.

Palmade, Guy P. *French Capitalism in the Nineteenth Century.* New York: Barnes & Noble, 1972.

Piettre, André. *Histoire économique: essai de synthèse faits et idées.* Paris: Éditions Cujas, 1969.

_____. *Monnaie et économie internationale du XIXe siècle à nos jours.* Paris: Éditions Cujas, [1967].

Pinkney, David H. *Napoleon III and the Rebuilding of Paris.* Princeton: Princeton University Press, 1958.

Plessis, Alain. *La Politique de la Banque de France de 1851 à 1870.* Genève: Droz, 1985.

Pomeroy, Earl S. "French Substitutes for American Cotton, 1861-1865." *Journal of Southern History* 9 (November 1943): 555-60.

Price, Roger. *An Economic History of Modern France 1730-1914.* Rev. ed. London: Macmillan, 1981.

Rippy, J. Fred. *Rivalry of the United States and Great Britain over Latin America, 1808-1830.* Baltimore: Johns Hopkins Press, 1929.

_____. "Mexican Projects of the Confederates." *Southwestern Historical Quarterly* 22 (April 1919): 291-317.

_____. *The United States and Mexico.* New York: F. S. Crofts, 1931.

Rist, Charles. *The Triumph of Gold.* Philip Cortney trans. of *La défense de l'or.* New York: Philosophical Library, 1961.

Rister, Carl Coke. "Carlota, A Confederate Colony in Mexico." *Journal of Southern History* 11 (February-November 1945): 33-50.

Robertson, William Spence. "The Tripartite Treaty of London." *Hispanic American Historical Review* 20 (May 1940): 167-89.

Rolle, Andrew F. *The Lost Cause: The Confederate Exodus to Mexico.* Norman: University of Oklahoma Press, 1965.

Schoonover, Thomas. "U.S. Economic Penetration into Mexico in the 1860's." A paper presented March 7, 1974 at the Missouri Valley History Conference, Omaha, Nebraska.

_____. "Dollars over Dominion: United States Economic Interests in Mexico, 1861-1867." *Pacific Historical Review* XLI, 1 (February 1976): 23-45.

Schramm, E. F. *Report on Artemisa Mines, Ltd.: Located in Sonora, Mexico, with a Description of the Ore Deposits.* Bisbee, Arizona: Stockholders Report to President Oliver Kendall, Artemisa Mines, Ltd., 1932.

Scroggs, William O. *Filibusters and Financiers: The Story of William Walker and His Associates.* New York: MacMillan, 1916.

Shaw, W. A. *The History of Currency: 1252 to 1896.* 2nd ed. London: Wilsons & Milne, 1896.

Sobarzo, Horacio. *Crónica de la aventura de Raousset-Boulbon en Sonora.* México: Librería de Manuel Porrúa, S.A., 1954.

Soetbeer, Adolf. *Edelmetall-Produktion und wertverhältniss zwischen gold und silber, seit der entdeckung Amerika's bis zur gegenwart.* Gotha: J. Perthes, 1879.

Soulié, Maurice. *The Wolf Cub: The Great Adventure of Count Gaston de Raousset-Boulbon in California and Sonora, 1850-1854.* Indianapolis: Bobbs-Merrill, 1927. First published in French (Paris 1926) from family documents.

Stevens, Robert C. "The Apache Menace in Sonora, 1831-1849." *Arizona and the West* 6 (Autumn 1964): 211-22.

Stout, Joseph Allen, Jr. *The Liberators: Filibustering Expeditions into Mexico, 1848-1862.* Los Angeles: Westernlore Press, 1973.

Stuart, H. W. "A Scarcity of Gold?" *Journal of Political Economy* 3 (June 1895): 362-65.

Thomas, Lately. *Between Two Empires: The Life Story of California's First Senator, William McKendree Gwin.* Boston: Houghton Mifflin, 1969.

Timmons, Wilbert H. *Morelos: Priest, Soldier, Statesman of Mexico.* El Paso: Western College Press, 1963.

Villa, Eduardo W. *Historia del Estado de Sonora.* 2nd ed. Hermosillo, Sonora: Editorial Sonora, 1951.

Voss, Stuart F. *On the Periphery of Nineteenth Century Mexico: Sonora and Sinaloa 1810-1877.* Tucson: University of Arizona Press, 1982.

White, Elizabeth Brett. *American Opinion of France: From Lafayette to Poincaré.* New York: Alfred A. Knopf, 1927.

White, Horace. "Bimetallism in France." *Political Science Quarterly* 6 (June 1891): 311-37.

Willis, Henry Parker. *A History of the Latin Monetary Union: A Study of International Monetary Action.* Chicago: University of Chicago Press, 1901.

_____. "The Operation of Bimetallism in France." *Journal of Political Economy* 3 (June 1895): 356-62.

Wolowski, Louis F. M.R. *L'or et l'argent*. Paris: Guillaumin et cie, 1870.

Wyllys, Rufus Kay. *The French in Sonora, 1850-1854: The Story of French Adventurers from California into Mexico*. Berkeley: University of California Press, 1932.

Zamacois, Niceto de. *Historia de Méjico desde sus tiempos mas remotos hasta nuestros días*. 18 vols. México and Barcelona: [1880-82]. Vol. 12.

Index

About the Author

Shirley J. Black

——————•———————

(1935-1996)

Shirley Jean (Ferrell) Black was born and raised in Tulsa, Oklahoma. She studied at Oklahoma State University, Baylor University, UCLA – Northridge and the University of Oklahoma, where she earned her doctorate in modern European history. Her research interests centered on the career of Louis Napoleon Bonaparte, Napoleon III. While at Texas A&M University she organized an innovative mentors program, won an award for teaching excellence and also a national award for counseling.